Hometown Heroines

Betty Bolté

Hometown Heroines

Betty Bolté

Writer's Showcase
San Jose New York Lincoln Shanghai

Hometown Heroines

Writer's Showcase
an imprint of iUniverse.com, Inc.

For information address:
iUniverse.com, Inc.
5220 S 16th, Ste. 200
Lincoln, NE 68512
www.iuniverse.com

ISBN: 0-595-16793-4

Printed in the United States of America

I couldn't have written this book
without the love and support of my family.

I dedicate this book to my children,
Danielle and Nicholas,
who read many of the stories
to make sure they were interesting.

To my father,
Robert M. Solomon, Sr.,
who threatened to publish it himself
if nobody else would.

But most of all to my husband, Chris,
for his love, support, and faith in my ability,
even as we traipsed through cemeteries
across the country
while he was supposed to be on vacation.

I love you all.

Contents

Acknowledgements xi

Introduction xv

Milly Cooper Brown 1

Mallee Francis 9

Joanna Troutman 20

Annie Ellsworth 34

Virginia Reed 43

Abigail Gardner 64

Jane Silcott 87

Grace Bedell Billings 95

Mary Kate Patterson 103

Belle Boyd 116

Nancy Crouse 137

Emma Sansom 150

Winnie Mae Murphree 165

Lavinia Ellen Ream 178

Kate Shelley 200

Sophie Bell Wright 216

Minnie Freeman 225

Edwina Fay Fuller 234

Lucille Mulhall 244

Index 259

LIST OF ILLUSTRATIONS

Cooper's Fort, Boonslick, Missouri. 2

Historical marker at the site of the fort. 4

Mallee pleads for McKrimmon's life. 11

Milly Francis' stone monument. 18

Portrait of Joanna Troutman. 21

Historical marker tells the story of Joanna Troutman. 25

Joanna Troutman's grave site. 30

Portrait of Annie Ellsworth. 35

Portrait of Virginia Reed. 60

Abigail Gardner's cabin. 65

Sketch of Abigail Gardner. 77

Portrait of Abigail Gardner Sharp. 83

Portrait of Jane Silcott. 89

Lincoln-Bedell Statue Park, Westfield, New York. 97

Plaque at Lincoln-Bedell Statue Park. 101

Mary Kate Patterson's home in La Vergne, Tennessee. 105

Portrait of Mary Kate Patterson. 107

Historical marker for Mary Kate Patterson Davis Hill Kyle. 111

Kate's grave marker. 113

Belle Boyd at 18 years old. 117

Portrait of Belle Boyd. 124

Nancy Crouse's house, Middletown, Maryland. 140

Portrait of Emma Sansom. 151

Base of Emma Sansom monument in Gadsden, Alabama. 153

Emma Sansom Monument in Gadsden, Alabama. 161
Portrait of Winnie Mae Murphree. 167
Portrait of Celia Murphree. 170
Historical marker for the Murphree sisters. 173
Winnie Mae Murphree Bynum's gravesite. 175
Vinnie Ream at 15 years old. 179
Vinnie Ream's museum exhibit. 182
Vinnie Ream's life-size Lincoln statue. 184
Vinnie Ream's life-size Farragut statue. 192
Vinnie Ream's grave with monument. 197
Kate Shelley at 15 years old. 202
The Kate Shelley High Bridge. 205
Kate Shelley's gravesite and memorial plaque. 212
The memorial plaque at Kate's grave. 214
Sophie Wright's statue in New Orleans, Louisiana. 219
Sophie B. Wright Middle School, New Orleans. 223
Minnie Freeman and students. 226
Portrait of Minnie Freeman. 228
Fay Fuller dressed for climbing Mt. Rainier. 236
Lucille Mulhall calling for time. 245
Mulhall town sign. 246
Lucille Mulhall ready to perform. 247
Historical marker in Mulhall, Oklahoma. 249
Lucille Mulhall. 251
Mulhall family grave marker. 253

ACKNOWLEDGEMENTS

Researching and writing this book has been an ongoing endeavor for more than seven years. Many people have helped me during that time. Librarians at various public libraries across the country answered my questions and provided copies of articles. The Interlibrary Borrowing Department at the Indiana University-Purdue University at Indianapolis Library processed my countless requests for books and articles.

I give my special thanks to Jenny Thompson, Karen Allen, Jane Lodge, and Damara Bolté, who edited and proofread the final manuscript before publication.

Thanks to Laura Crane and Anita Prewitt, researchers, for digging up little-known facts in Missouri and Texas.

Thanks also to the following individuals at historical societies who helped me gather copies of articles and photos: Elaine Miller, Washington State Historical Society; Mr. Lloyd Geiger, Boonslick Historical Society; Charles Irwin, Boone County (Iowa) Historical Society; Marie Concannon, State Historical Society of Missouri; Joan Morris and Samuel Burns, Florida State Archives; John Anderson, Texas State Library and Archives Commission; Lucinda Long, Nevada Humanities Committee; Matthew Schaefer, State Historical Society of Iowa; Troy Reeves, Idaho State Historical Society. Special thanks to Mrs. Wanda Norton, Curator at the Eastern Trails Museum in Vinita, Oklahoma for opening the display case so my husband could take photos of Vinnie's artifacts.

I'd like to thank the following people for granting permission to quote from their work. (Please check the individual stories for the complete citation.) Quotes pertaining to the story of Joanna Troutman are reprinted by permission of Edward R. Vinson from his book, *Texas' Betsy Ross and the Men of Goliad* (1985). A few short quotes in the story about Virginia Reed, taken from *The Donner Party Chronicles* (1997) by Frank Mullen, Jr., are used by permission of the Nevada Humanities Committee. The letters written by Grace Bedell and Abraham Lincoln are quoted with permission from the *Wichita Eagle*, Wichita, Kansas. The letter Belle Boyd wrote to her cousin Willie is quoted with permission of *The Washington Times*. Nancy Crouse's reply to the officer holding a gun to her head is quoted from George C. Rhoderick's *The Early History of Middletown Maryland*. Nancy Crouse's ballad is quoted from *Middletown Valley in Song and Story* with permission by the Central Maryland Heritage League. Fay Fuller's feelings as she climbed Mt. Rainier are quoted with permission by *Columbia Magazine*.

Additionally, I've quoted from several public domain works. Several comments, as well as the initial sketch of Abigail Gardner have been used from her book, *History of the Spirit Lake Massacre, March 8, 1857* (1895). The conversation between Annie Ellsworth and Samuel Morse is quoted from *Samuel F.B. Morse: His Letters and Journals* (1973), edited by Edward Lind Morse and printed by Da Capo Press, Inc. I also quoted Belle Boyd from her book, *Belle Boyd in Camp in Prison* (1865). "A Ballad of Emma Sansom," by John Trotwood Moore, is quoted from *The Blue and the Gray: The Best Poems of the Civil War* (1943). The photos of the Murphree sisters appeared in the *Alabama Reunion Edition of the Heritage of Blount County* (1989).

I'd like to thank Ms. Ernestine Fergus for showing me—a perfect stranger—the inside of Mary Kate Patterson Davis Hill Kyle's home in LaVergne, Tennessee.

Glenn Sherwood, author of *A Labor of Love*, read and commented on my interpretation of Vinnie Ream's life. Thank you for your insights and corrections.

Mrs. Deanna Agan, president of the Kate Shelley Doll Club, provided additional research I hadn't uncovered. Thank you for your interest and support. Thanks to Winona Mylenbusch Decker for allowing me to include the song, "Kate Shelley: The Girl Who Saved the Train."

Thanks to Sherri Whorton, President of the Emma Sansom Chapter of the United Daughters of the Confederacy #2564 in Rome, Georgia, for providing information from the chapter's files.

Thanks also to the teachers—Barbara Pace, Joan Meek, Jeanne Mattingly, and Pam Fischer—who have read and shared these stories with their classes. Thanks for the encouragement to follow my dream.

INTRODUCTION

If you enjoy reading about the lives of others, and enjoy reading historical fiction, then I hope you'll love reading these stories about real young people and how they touched the hearts of their hometowns.

You won't find stories of the childhoods of famous adults. That's not who these girls are. These girls range in age from 7 to 20 years old. (I know, 20 is stretching the definition of *girl*, but I hope you'll agree that those girls were worth including.)

For the most part, the historical fiction story combines many sources of information. In some cases, notably the Murphree sisters and Milly Cooper, I could find very little information written down and accessible.

Because I used my research, personal experience, and imagination to write parts of these stories, I also included a "Just the Facts" section in each biography. That's where you'll see only the facts as I found them, with occasionally a dispute between sources noted.

Some of the girls had books written about them. Others had articles in magazines and newspapers. Some had ballads or songs composed for them. Some had poems written about them. You'll find what fiction and nonfiction books, movies, and other media are available for each girl in the "Check It Out!" section of the biography.

I searched the Internet for online sources and sites prior to printing this book, and those that I found of interest I've included in the "Web Sites and Online Resources" sections. Please do your own searches on those girls you're interested in, as I'm sure the sites will change. I can't guarantee these URLs will work when you try them, but I hope so because they have some wonderful photos and information.

In the "Wait 'Til You See This!" sections, you'll find places where you can go visit and feel closer to each of these girls. You might want to visit a park, or a bridge, or a monument on a busy street. A quiet moment or two in a museum's gallery will let you see specific items that the girls owned.

In case you find you want to do your own research, I've also included in the "Other Sources" sections any additional references I used in compiling these stories.

To set the stage a bit, the following timeline lists inventions that first appeared during the 19th century. A quick scan down the list will show you a glimpse of how life must have been for these heroines:

1807   Fulton's paddle steamer *Clermont* travels Hudson River

1816   Camera; Knitting Machine

1820   Elastic

1821   Electric motor

1826   First railroad in the United States

1829   First bus in New York

1830   First American steam locomotive, *Tom Thumb*, races horse-drawn railcar in Baltimore

1834   Refrigeration

1836   Phosphorous matches

1839   Velocipede (it came before the bicycle)

1840   Postage stamp

1843   Typing machine

1846   Artificial limbs

1854   Photographic roll films

1860   Can opener

1861   Barbed wire fence

1866   Dynamite

1868   First practical typewriter; plastics

1875   Submarine

1876   Telephone

1877   Phonograph, Bicycle popular

1878   Electric light introduced

1880   Inoculation

1884   Motor car

1885   Motorcycle

1886   Aluminum

1890   Rubber tires on bicycles for first time

1895   X-ray

1896   Radio

1897   Cold cereals

1899   Aspirin Magnetic tape recorder

I hope you enjoy these stories and that you find these girls as inspiring as I did.

MILLY COOPER BROWN

1812

Saving the Day

Milly stepped out of the tiny log cabin. The March sun hung just above the rows of upright poles that formed the stockade surrounding the cluster of cabins. Small, white clouds dotted the sky. She smiled at the beautiful sunrise.

"Enjoying the morning, daughter?"

Milly turned at the sound of her father's voice. Captain Braxton Cooper stood tall and confident beside her, with just a hint of worry in his eyes. She knew that as commander of the fort there were a lot of concerns for him to handle.

"Yes, Pa," she said, keeping her smile. "Seems hard to believe them Indians are planning to attack."

"I know. You stay safe inside the fort, you hear?"

"Yes, Pa."

"It's time I spoke to the families here about what we should do. Run and tell your Uncle Sarshell to get the families together."

"Yes, Pa." Milly strode into the morning sunshine. A few birds flew past, calling to each other. A meeting of the entire fort meant serious business. She lengthened her stride, kicking up clouds of dust around her long heavy skirts.

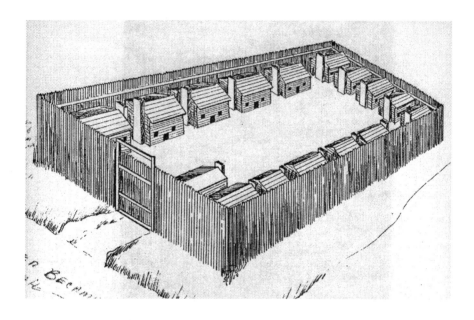

Cooper's Fort, Boonslick, Missouri. Courtesy of Boonslick Historical Society.

At 18 years old, Milly knew the dangers of living on the Missouri prairie. Between the severe weather and the tough soil to farm, it was a hard life for a young girl trying to grow up. Many days were spent outside the stockade walls, plowing, planting, and harvesting. There were no schools, so Milly learned from experience rather than books and teachers.

The Indians sometimes stole their horses, and gave them a hard time when they tried to get them back. Until the War of 1812 broke out, the Indians had been friendly. Then the British stepped in and turned them against the Americans. Since then, families living on the prairie and in the fort never knew when they might be attacked.

Milly approached her uncle's cabin. She told him that her pa wanted to have a meeting with all the families about what to do next. Before long, the families gathered in the meeting space in the center of the fort, between the cabins. Captain Cooper stood in the middle of the crowd of families. Milly, standing to one side, noted the lack of men inside the fort. Her uncle, Benjamin Cooper, had organized 250 of the men into a fighting unit called the Boonslick Rangers, and they were out fighting the Indians in different parts of the surrounding area. The women and children looked trustingly at her pa.

"There's a hostile band of Indians surrounding the fort," Captain Cooper said slowly. "We must prepare ourselves for a fierce attack, which can come at any time. The Rangers won't be back for weeks. After discussing our situation with my scouts, we feel we must try to get to Fort Hempstead to ask for help."

Fort Hempstead was a good many miles away, but because the Indians were between Fort Cooper and Fort Hempstead, it made the miles seem even farther. Tension had increased in recent weeks, with more attacks and bad feelings from the Indians. Milly knew her father needed a volunteer. She waited to see what the families would suggest.

"If any of the men here leave," said one woman, "who will protect us when the Indians attack?"

"We'll still have a few men here," Captain Cooper said. "But someone must go, or we are doomed." He gazed at each person in the crowd, until each looked away.

Milly straightened her shoulders and stepped forward.

"I'll go, Pa." She held her head high and looked him square in the eyes. "I'll ride to Fort Hempstead."

A murmur arose in the crowd surrounding Milly and her pa. Milly's friends gathered around her, upset that she would risk her life, yet knowing she was their best hope.

Captain Cooper took only a second to decide, trusting his daughter's riding ability and her natural bravery. He also knew the Indians waited just outside the walls of the fort.

"Saddle the fastest horse we have," he commanded.

Once Milly was seated atop the eager horse, Captain Cooper laid his hand on her knee and asked, "Milly, is there anything else that you want?"

"Only a spur, father," she answered.

As she trotted toward the gates, two men threw them open. She spurred her horse into a gallop. Once outside, she heard a hundred Indians holler their war cry as they attempted to stop her. The gates banged shut behind her.

She was on her own. The lives of the people at the fort depended solely on her horse carrying her to the woods and beyond to Fort Hempstead. Rifles fired from across the 200 yards of open prairie as she dashed toward the forest. She rode low and urged the animal on, ignoring the deadly whir of bullets as they passed near her.

Historical marker at the site of the fort as it appeared in 1997. Photo by Betty Bolté.

Soon she galloped into the forest, laying close to her horse's neck to avoid the sting of branches. The Indians turned their attention on the fort. Milly pressed her horse forward, riding as hard as she dared through the trees. She heard the increased fighting behind her and hoped she could bring help in time. The horse darted and swerved around trees, splashed through a creek, and up a steep bank. Crashing finally out of the underbrush, she rode up to the gates of Fort Hempstead. She had a quick exchange with the guards and the gates opened for her. She rode inside and slipped from the saddle, her horse lathered in sweat. She patted its neck. A crowd gathered around her and she explained the desperate situation at Fort Cooper. The men grabbed their guns and mounted their horses. Milly swung into the saddle again, and reined her horse toward the gates.

"Ready?" she called. Without waiting for an answer, she spurred her horse into a gallop and the rescue party thundered out of the fort. They raced back to Fort Cooper, startling birds into flight. As they approached the clearing between the forest and the fort, the Sioux saw them. With a whoop, the Sioux fled the area rather than stay and face the greater threat. Soon the gates swung open as the settlers inside realized the shooting had stopped. Milly led the rescue party into Fort Cooper. A cheer rose from the tired settlers.

Captain Cooper swung his daughter from the saddle and hugged her. "You're a hero, Milly. A true hero."

Milly just smiled.

Just the Facts

Mildred Cooper was born in 1796, in Madison County, Kentucky. Her father was Braxton Cooper. I didn't find any mention of her mother's name. In 1810 her father and uncles established Fort Cooper in what is now Franklin County, Missouri.

Milly had several brothers, but the sources I located didn't detail which of the Cooper men were related to each other. One handwritten source says the following Coopers moved from Fort Boonburgh, Madison County, Kentucky. Because Braxton Cooper, Sr. is Milly's father, presumably the last three Coopers in this list are Milly's brothers:

Lieut. Col. Benjamin Cooper
Francis Cooper
William Cooper
Daniel Cooper
John Cooper
Capt. Sarshell Cooper
Braxton Cooper, Sr.
Stephen Cooper
Braxton Cooper, Jr.
Robert Cooper

During the War of 1812, the British convinced the Indians that the American white men were their enemies. The Indians wanted the Americans off their land. As tensions escalated, Braxton Cooper, commander of Fort Cooper, brought together the families at the fort and told them they needed to send for help from Fort Hempstead. No one was willing to go, and then Milly stepped forward.

One source says that after Milly left the fort and rode to Fort Hempstead for help—nine miles away—the Indians doubled their attack on the fort. Just as the settlers inside the fort ran low on ammunition, the shooting outside the fort stopped and the Indians retreated. The settlers could see Milly leading a large group of pioneer fighters toward them. She had completed her mission and became the "Heroine of Fort Cooper." She is described as "a sprightly and vigorous frontier girl, having few of the graces of modern education" and "symmetrical in proportion and remarkable for cool and resolute daring in cases of great emergency, of which many instances might be given."

One of the other settlers at the fort was Robert Brown, whom Milly married in approximately 1816 at Fort Cooper. Robert had also come with the Coopers from Kentucky. They lived in the fort for about three years before moving to a farm east of Fayette, Missouri. According to the

1850 Census, they had two children, Frances (born 1825) and David (born 1834), both of Missouri.

According to the 1860 Census, Milly and Robert operated a boarding house of some type, and it was fairly successful as their net worth is listed as $6000—about five times their neighbor's net worth.

Milly Cooper Brown died November 5, 1869 and was buried in the family cemetery.

Check It Out!

McDaniel, Lyn, ed. *Bicentennial Boonslick History*. First printing Jan 1976; Second printing Aug 1987. Boonslick: 1976 Boonslick Historical Society, 611 6th Street, Boonville, MO 65233.

"Mildred Cooper Brown." Pioneer Women in Missouri History. *Show Me Missouri Women*. Volume 2. Published by the Missouri Historical Society.

Wait 'Til You See This!

An historical marker erected in 1984 by The Boonslick Historical Society stands proudly where Fort Cooper used to be. The marker is located on Z highway, about 14 miles from I-70. To get there, from I-70 near Boonville, MO, turn north on Route 87 to Route 5, then to Route 87 again, then turn on Highway Z and go past Highway J by a half mile.

The marker says, in part:

> *Site of largest and most important of the Boon's Lick forts during War of 1812. Built on a slight rise, the stronghold and center of defense consisted of a group of log cabins placed closely together and*

encircled by a log stockade. It covered about 3 acres of land. Cleared fields lay between the stockade and the woods.

In Centralia, Missouri, the local chapter of the Daughters of the American Revolution is called the Milly Brown Chapter (#3-098-Mo). The chapter's organizing regent, Emma Jean Brown Ballew, was Milly's great-great-granddaughter.

Other Sources

Foley, William E. *The Genesis of Missouri: From Wilderness Outpost to Statehood.* 221-229. Columbia: University of Missouri Press, 1989.

Lay, William D. *Indian Trade Factories and Forts in the Boonslick 1812-1815.* Manuscript, 1995.

Sherr, Lynn and Jurate Kazickas. *Susan B. Anthony Slept Here: A Guide to American Women's Landmarks.* 246-7. New York: Random House, 1994.

MALLEE FRANCIS

1818

To Save Her Enemy's Life

Spring had just arrived in Florida. It was almost the end of March when Mallee walked with her sister to the gentle river gurgling beneath willow trees. She fingered her tunic decorated with beads and feathers, enjoying the familiar feel of it in her hand, yet wishing she could wear the fine dresses laying neatly in the trunk at home. The lavish gift from her father's English friends evoked much jealousy among the other women in the Creek tribe. So she only wore them when she went with her British friend, Robert Ambrister, to visit the Spanish fort. Her father had received a British general's uniform, sparkling in gold buttons and braid, along with a golden hatchet. The trunk had arrived filled to the brim with satin, lace, corsets, bonnets, and more. To avoid trouble among her people, she saved the dresses for visits to Fort St. Marks with her father, Chief Francis the Prophet.

Mallee was an Indian princess, and she fit the part perfectly. Her horsemanship surpassed all others. She could stand on the ground and leap onto the back of her horse and ride off, as easily as if she sat on a chair.

Mallee's sister stopped at the river's edge and picked up a flat, smooth stone. With a flick of her wrist, she sent it skipping across the calm river.

"Four hops. I bet you can't beat that!" she cried.

Without a word, Mallee selected a rock from the path and sent it hopping across the water. "Seven."

"Lucky. I'll try again." The older sister searched for another rock. "Why did you tell those women at the fort you married Robert?"

Mallee thought about the tall, handsome man. He had given her many fine gifts of clothing, but he was already engaged to a woman waiting for him in England. Mallee knew Robert was a very good friend, and that was all.

Mallee chuckled. "To make them squirm, why else?" Robert loved to help her play jokes on the other women.

"How did he like it?"

"He laughed of course."

Suddenly, a whoop echoed through the trees, announcing the arrival of a war party back to the village of Francistowne. Mallee's father founded the town in 1814, along the Wakulla River in western Florida. Mallee heard the commotion echoing and ran back to town. Since General Andrew Jackson had returned to Spanish Florida at the beginning of the year, the tribes had grown increasingly fearful of the American soldiers. It had become harder for Francis to control his warriors. Mallee hurried past her father's house and into the clearing.

Already the rest of her people had gathered in the circle. At the center, a young white man twisted and turned, trying to hide his nakedness from the hostile Indians. Mallee strode up beside her father and watched, afraid for the boy.

He can't be much older than myself, she thought, maybe 17 summers. He couldn't be any threat to our tribes, he is not old enough to know what war is all about. Why have they captured him? She knew that among the Indians an agreement had been "given out" that the life of any white men caught by an Indian was totally in the hands of that Indian.

Mallee pleads for McKrimmon's life. Courtesy Florida State Archives Photographic Collections.

"Father, it is a pity this young man should die when he has no head for war," Mallee said urgently to her father. "You must stop them."

"It is out of my hands, daughter," her father replied.

"But you are the Chief!"

"You must take your pleas to them," Francis said, raising a hand toward the angry Indians dancing around the white man. "Go to the men who have the right over the young man's life."

Mallee ran across the clearing to the two Indians and pleaded with them to spare the white man. "Do not shoot him! He is too young to have a head for war!"

One of them turned to her, his face contorted with rage. "He should die, for my two sisters were killed by white men! Go."

Mallee tugged on his arm to draw his attention back to her. "Killing this white man will not bring back your sisters. He is but a boy! He has not the head of a man to guide him. Spare his life."

The Indians gazed at Mallee for a moment, then at the young man still tied to the stake. Mallee waited, uncertain in what direction their thoughts would take them.

"If he will live among us and not try to leave, and wear his hair like us, then his life will be spared."

Nodding, Mallee hurried to the young man. He twisted away from her, trying yet to hide himself from view. "If you will allow your head to be shaved and promise to live among us without trying to escape, they will spare your life. Do you agree?"

The man thrust his head out toward her. "Yes, yes, cut it all off if you choose!"

Mallee told the other Indians what he'd said, and he was immediately cut loose. His head was thrust forward and his hair shaved off from the sides, leaving only a straight strip down the middle. Then they set him loose and he was given clothes and moccasins.

Once he was dressed, Mallee took him to her tepee and gave him some food to eat.

"What is your name?" she asked, as she set a bowl in front of him.

"Captain Duncan McKrimmon," he said, "of the Georgia militia, second regiment."

"With General Jackson?" Mallee asked. He really was the enemy, then.

"Yes. You speak English very well," Duncan said. "How is that possible?"

"My father supports the British in their fight against the Americans," she said. "I have learned through that friendship."

"And do you have a name?" Duncan asked.

"My people call me Mallee," she said, "but the English call me Milly."

"Thank you for your help this afternoon, Milly," Duncan said. "I surely would have died without your help."

"You are too young to be much of a threat to us," she said candidly.

"How old are you then," he asked, smiling, "if I'm too young?"

"I have lived fifteen summers," Milly said proudly.

Duncan told Milly how Jackson's troops had just settled in at the new Fort Gadsden on the Apalachicola River and were waiting for more forces to join them from Tennessee. Growing bored, Duncan had been given permission by his commander to go fishing. It was while he was fishing that the Indians captured him, bound him, and dragged him back to the village. They stripped off his uniform and tied him to the post. The rest Milly knew first hand.

"You'll be safe now as long as you don't try to leave," she told him. She poured him some water from a skin bag and he gratefully drank it.

During the next few days, Milly and Duncan became good friends, despite being on opposite sides in the war. Then the day came when Duncan was traded back to the commandant at Fort St. Marks in exchange for seven and a half gallons of rum. Milly missed her new friend, but she was glad that he had survived his fishing trip.

Life settled back to normal for Milly and her family. One day a large ship cruised up the river and anchored nearby, the British Union Jack fluttering in the breeze. Milly watched from shore as Chief Francis and a neighboring chief named Himollimico approached the ship in small boats, expecting to receive supplies from the British. Chief Francis appeared in his best clothes: a gray frock coat, top hat, loin cloth, and moccasins. They were invited aboard by the captain and went below deck.

Milly approached the ship in a second canoe that was paddled by a brave. Milly heard the captain order the crew to fire on the canoe. The shots landed around the canoe. Milly ducked down, but not before seeing her friend Duncan watching from the rail of the ship. Milly held onto the side of the canoe as the brave spun the canoe in the water and paddled them to safety.

Milly was surprised at the sudden turn of events in her life. Her father had been captured, her friend had betrayed her and her people despite her saving his life. She could only hope events would sort themselves out for her people's benefit.

Just the Facts

Mallee Francis was the princess daughter of Creek Chief Francis the Prophet, also known as Hillis Hadjo (meaning "unreasonably courageous"). Of that much, all accounts agree. However, more research showed varying stories as to how and when Mallee saved Duncan McKrimmon. The following is as accurate as is possible to conclude.

In 1813 Francis the Prophet was forced to leave his home in Alabama Territory and he established a new town on the Wakulla River, just above Fort St. Marks. It was first known as Francis Towne, then Cypress Creek Village, and today as Pine Arbor. Until 1818 life was relatively fair and just to the Creeks and Seminoles living there.

Then in 1818 General Andrew Jackson led his army in Spanish Florida to settle the restless Seminoles in what became known as the First Seminole War. Hostilities between the Americans and the Seminoles continued to increase as the year went by.

At the end of March, two Seminole Indians captured Duncan McKrimmon, a 17-year-old member of the Georgia Militia. Some accounts merely say he was a "member," others say he was a "captain." One account says he was just a boy fishing along the creek, while another says he was sort of an errand boy for the Georgia militia. Whatever his rank, he was with the Georgia militia, he did go fishing, and he was captured by Indians and taken to Francistown.

Mallee, or Milly as English-speaking people called her, was 15 years old when she and her sister were playing on the bank of the river and heard the warriors' whoop as they brought Duncan into town. She pleaded with her father first, then with the two braves, for Duncan's life and won his freedom on the condition he shave his head and live among them. He agreed. Most likely he only stayed there several days, rather than the two years one account reports, because the incidents he was involved in all happened during the spring and summer of 1818. He was exchanged for a barrel of whiskey or 7½ gallons of rum, again depending on which story you want to believe.

Two American ships sailed into the St. Marks harbor flying British flags to trick Francis the Prophet on board and secure his capture. He was hanged on April 8, 1818 by order of General Jackson. It is said he had a knife hidden up his sleeve. Robert Ambrister, Milly's friend, was shot on April 29, 1818 as Milly and others watched. His execution distressed the young woman for a long time.

On approximately August 27, 1818, 188 starving Indians from Francistown surrendered to Lieutenant Colonel Arbuckle, the commander at Fort Gadsden, Florida. Milly was among them.

In December 1818, Duncan located Milly at Fort Gadsden. Seeing the miserable condition she was in—starving and poor—he proposed marriage to her in an effort to save her. She refused him saying "she did not save his life to marry him."

The Creeks and Seminoles were moved to Oklahoma in 1820. Here the trail of Milly's life becomes hard to follow. It is said she married a Creek man and had eight children, three of whom survived. One of her descendants, Charles Sakim Daniels, started a museum in her honor in Wakulla Springs, Florida, in the mid-1980s. The museum has since been closed.

Colonel Ethan Allen Hitchcock visited Milly in her home in Oklahoma on January 27, 1842. Her house was in the shadow of Fort Gibson at Muskogee. She had become a devout Baptist during her life out west. She was destitute and struggling to survive. Hitchcock recorded her story in his journal, and upon his return to Washington, D.C., he recommended to the U.S. Government that she receive compensation for her heroic act during the war. Congress passed an act on June 17, 1844, granting her a pension of $96 per year, and called for a medal to be made.

Be it enacted...That the Secretary of War be, and he is hereby authorized and directed to pay to Milly, an Indian woman of the Creek nation, and daughter of the prophet Francis, a pension at the rate of ninety-six dollars per annum, payable semi-annually during her natural life, as a testimonial of the gratitude and bounty of the United States, for the humanity displayed by her in the war of one thousand eight hundred and seventeen and one thousand eight hundred and eighteen in saving the life of an American citizen, who was a prisoner in the hands of her people and about to be put to death by them; the said pension to commence and take effect from the fourth day of September, one thousand eight hundred and forty-three.

Section 2. And it is further enacted, That the Secretary of War be, and he is hereby authorized and directed to procure, and transmit to the said Milly, a medal with appropriate devices impressed thereon, of the value of not exceeding twenty dollars, as an additional testimonial of the gratitude of the United States.

Approved June 17, 1844.

It wasn't until June 1847, though, that the Commissioner of Indian Affairs was able to carry out the provisions of the act. The delay in the pension and in creating the medal spanned four years from the time the act was passed.

Milly meanwhile was losing her struggle to survive. Her hard life had weakened her resistance and she contracted tuberculosis. When the Creek Agent went to deliver the paperwork that she needed to sign to receive her pension, he found her in bed, dying. He made sure a doctor came to her and that everything possible was done to make her comfortable. She never saw a penny of the pension; however, her family did. By all accounts, the medal was never made.

Milly Francis died on May 19, 1848 at approximately 45 years of age. She is buried "somewhere between the city limits of Muskogee, Oklahoma and the Arkansas river."

Check It Out!

Foreman, Grant, ed. *A Traveler in Indian Territory: The Journal of Ethan Allen Hitchcock, late Major-General in the United States Army*. Cedar Rapids: The Torch Press, 1930.

You can get more information by contacting the Florida State Archives, R.A. Gray Building, Tallahassee, Florida 32399-0250, (904) 487-2073.

Online Resources

To learn more about the War of 1812, go to *http://members.home.net/gronj /service.htm*. There you will find, under the subtitle "Florida," information on the events surrounding Milly's brave act.

The engraved sketch shown earlier originally appeared in Henry Trumbull's 1802 book, *History of the Discovery of America*. The book is held by the University of Miami's Richter Library in The Helen Carmichael Purdy Foundation collection. To view parts of this book, go to *www.library.miami.edu/archives/Purdy/purdy_trumbull.htm*.

Wait 'Til You See This!

Stone marker at Bacone College, Muskogee, Oklahoma. Photo by Betty Bolté.

The senior class of Bacone College (1933) erected a stone monument in 1934 between the chapel and the Ataloa Lodge, Bacone College, Muskogee, Oklahoma.

Other Sources

Davis, T. Frederick. "Milly Francis and Duncan McKrimmon: An Authentic Florida Pocahontas." *Florida Historical Quarterly*. Copy received from Historical Society without further identification.

Heidler, David S. and Jeanne T. Heidler. *Old Hickory's War: Andrew Jackson and the Quest for Empire*. Mechanicsburg: Stackpole Books, 1996.

Information received from the offices of Bacone College, Muskogee, OK.

Miller, Lou Whitfield. "Mallee." Manuscript of article appearing in the *Tallahassee Historical Society Annual*, 1937.

Sherr, Lynn and Jurate Kazickas. *Susan B. Anthony Slept Here: A Guide to American Women's Landmarks*. 368. New York: Random House, 1994.

Stiggins, George. *Creek Indian History: A Historical Narrative of the Genealogy, Traditions and Downfall of the Ispocoga or Creek Indian Tribe of Indians, by One of the Tribe*. Edited by Virginia Pounds Brown. Birmingham: Birmingham Public Library Press, 1989.

Unsigned letter addressed to "Dear Friend" and used as marketing material for The Museum, about Milly Francis. Dated January 12, 1983.

West, C. W. 'Dub'. "Theories abound on Creek Pocahontas." *Muskogee Phoenix*. Life section, "Turning Back Clock," June 1997.

Woodruff, Lee. "Milly Francis: Florida's Pocahontas." *Tallahassee Magazine*. Summer 1981.

Joanna Troutman

1836

The Lone Star

Sweeping the hardwood floor of the inn was no fun, Joanna thought, taking an extra swipe with the broom. She looked up to see her father's gentle eyes on her. She knew he was proud of his roadside inn, the Troutman Inn, and that he wanted the dining room and bedrooms to be clean and welcoming. The two-story building was a resting spot for people traveling on horseback and stagecoach, a place to have a drink, a bite to eat and, if needed, a bed to sleep on. She smiled and went back to her work, collecting the never-ending dirt into a pile to be swept out the door. She brushed back a stray wisp of black hair that had escaped from her braid and sighed. Sometimes she wished she could do something more important than clean and cook for the guests each evening.

"Jo, would you get some fresh linens for the rooms upstairs. We have more guests this evening," her father said. Joanna had noticed a group of dusty men and women who had arrived earlier by stagecoach, and suspected they'd be staying.

"Of course, father," Joanna said. She set aside her broom and hurried across the large dining room. Gathering her long skirts in one hand, she skipped up the wooden stairs. She turned down the hall and opened the door to the second bedroom on the left. The room boasted a double bed covered in down comforters and feather pillows. An oak desk and chair stood before the window, allowing the guest to look out at the woods behind the inn. After making up the beds with clean white sheets, she checked each room to be sure each was ready. Satisfied, she walked back downstairs.

The door to the inn opened as she reached the last step. A group of soldiers came in and sat down at a table. Joanna noticed one man in particular. His broad shoulders and easy manner gave him an air of confidence that she immediately liked.

Joanna Troutman's portrait hangs in the Texas State Capitol. Courtesy of Texas State Library & Archives Commission.

Mr. Troutman approached the table as they made themselves comfortable. "A whiskey, if you don't mind," the tall man said to Joanna's father.

The deep tone of his voice, combined with the way he spoke, sent a shiver through Joanna. She tried to avoid looking at him, but her eyes were drawn to him. She didn't want to be too forward, but she kept tabs on what he did and said. Suddenly, his eyes met hers. She looked away, returning to her sweeping to escape his gaze. But she could feel his gaze as she worked her way around the room. What did he think of her? Did he like her pale skin, her brown eyes, her quirky upturned nose? Or did he think she was just a child at 17 years old? She shook herself to stop her thoughts.

"Miss?" the man said. "Could I trouble you for a bite to eat?"

Joanna noticed the handsome man watching her. His smile melted her fears of being too young or not pretty enough.

"I'll be right back," she said, with a nod. She hurried into the kitchen and prepared a plate of fried chicken, peas, and corn bread.

"That smells wonderful," he said as she set the plate on the table in front of him. He looked at her. "May I ask your name?"

"Joanna Troutman. My father over there—his name is Hiram Troutman, and he owns this inn," she said with a smile. "And you, sir, what is your name?"

"Lieutenant Hugh McLeod, at your service," Hugh said with a slight bow.

"Are you going to Texas then?" Joanna's interest was sparked by the knowledge that Hugh was in the military. And since he was in Knoxville, he must be on his way to fight for the freedom of those Americans who had settled in the Mexican province of Texas.

"Yes, Joanna," Hugh said. "I'm to lead a group of volunteers from Macon and Columbus in a few days."

"The settlers will be glad to see you and your men," Joanna said. "But, you're starving." She motioned to his meal. "Please, eat."

Hugh nodded and started to eat, his attention returning to his comrades at the table. Joanna moved to the kitchen doorway, reluctant to leave, yet knowing she was expected home soon. Her father walked up to her as she leaned against the door.

"A fine group of soldiers," he said. "But it's time for you to head home before it gets too late. We don't want your mother to worry."

Soon Joanna was riding toward Elmwood, her family's plantation home. She watched the grove of elm trees surrounding the house loom larger as her mount neared the two-story house with its many woodfire chimneys sending smoke toward the stars.

While preparing for bed, she thought about Hugh McLeod—his voice, his manners, his strength—and hoped she'd see him again.

For the next three evenings, Joanna was pleased to see Hugh come into the inn for supper. He always spoke to her. She looked for him, wanting to know more about him. She found out that he'd resigned his commission from the United States Army in order to fight for the Americans in Texas. He was from Georgia and he was 21 years old. Joanna wasn't sure how her parents would react to him being four years older than her, but she hoped they wouldn't mind. Would he come back from Texas? She wondered whether she would ever see him once he left to take the volunteers across country.

On the fourth evening, Hugh held her hand in his as they sat together on the east verandah of the inn. The sky was clear, a gentle breeze stirring the moss hanging from the live oak trees nearby. She smelled the honeysuckle that edged the property. With Hugh holding her hand, she felt like a woman.

"Hugh, what really made you want to fight in Texas?" Joanna asked. "I mean, not everyone would give up a career to fight for people they don't even know."

"Well, Jo, I believe in freedom for everyone to live meaningful lives," he said. "You see that star up there—the North Star?"

"Yes." Joanna looked up at the bright star shining in the deepening black sky, with a faint cloud of stars stretching across the heavens.

"The Anglos who have moved to Texas live under the same stars we are gazing at here in Georgia," he said. "I believe that their government, the United States, should continue to protect them. But if the government won't, then it's up to us who live in the South to put our lives on the line for them."

"I just wish there were something I could do," Joanna said, with a small shrug. "I want to be a part of this in some way."

Hugh gazed at her for a moment, then back at the sky. "There's one way you can help."

"How?" Joanna asked.

"We don't have a flag to lead us into battle. Perhaps you could make one for us."

"A flag! Yes. But when do you leave?"

"In three days."

"Gracious. That's not much time. I'd better begin working on it."

"I must return to camp, as well." Hugh stood and helped Joanna rise to her feet. "I'll see you later, Jo." He squeezed her hand gently with his rough one. With a nod of farewell, he walked down the steps and mounted his horse. As the hoofbeats faded into the night, Joanna looked again at the North Star.

"A star!" she cried. She could see in her mind's eye what her flag would look like—a white background with one lone blue star in the middle. Beneath the star on one side would be the words "Liberty or Death," and on the other "where liberty dwells, there is my country." Excited, she hurried home to find fabric to make the flag.

Two days later she rode happily to the inn, carrying her prized possession. She had used one of her white silk skirts to make the flag, and cut up a second blue silk skirt to make the star on each side. As she had thought about the mottos, it occured to her to put the second one into Latin. With the help of a Latin dictionary, she translated the motto—*Ubi Libertas Habitat Ibi Patria Est*. Then she embroidered both mottos onto the flag. She was pleased with the way it had turned out, and she couldn't wait to show Hugh.

Historical marker located near where the inn stood in Knoxville, Georgia. Photo by Betty Bolté.

But he didn't come into the inn that night. She rode home with a heavy heart. The next day, however, she was at the inn early, because Hugh had told her the volunteers were riding out that morning. Again, Hugh wasn't there. But she saw his commander, Lieutenant Colonel William Ward, leading the mounted men down the main road past the inn. He could help her! She ran into the street, clutching her flag to her.

"Colonel Ward!" she called. The colonel reined in his horse and halted the troops.

"Yes, Miss?" he asked.

"Where is Lieutenant McLeod?"

"I've sent him ahead to help the recruiting in Columbus," he said, smiling gently. "I'm sorry he didn't have chance to say good-bye before he left."

"He asked me to make a flag," she said. She unfolded it and held it up for the men to see. "Would you take it and show it to the lieutenant when you arrive in Columbus?" She hesitated, then added, "And fly it in front of your army?"

Colonel Ward leaned down from his horse to take the flag, then he squeezed her hand in gratitude.

"Please tell him to be careful, and that I hope we meet again," Joanna said.

"I will." Colonel Ward signaled his troops and they started down the road at a brisk trot.

A week passed without any word. For Joanna, it was a long week. Finally, a letter arrived from Hugh. He'd written on November 23, 1835 from the camp in Columbus, Georgia.

Miss Troutman:

Col. Ward brought your handsome and appropriate flag as a present to the Georgia Volunteers in the cause of "Texas and Liberty." I was fearful with the shortness of time, you would not be able to finish it as tastefully as you would wish, but I assure you without any emotion of flattery, that it is beautiful and with us its value is enhanced by the recollection of the donor.

I thank you for the honor of being made the medium of presentation to the company and if they are what every true Georgian ought to be, our flag shall yet wave over fields of victory against despotism. I hope the proud day may soon arrive and while your star presides, no one can doubt our success.

Very respectfully your friend,
Hugh McLeod

Joanna read and read the letter, memorizing each word. Not only had she helped the brave men in her own small way, but Hugh thought the flag beautiful. She smiled as she folded the letter and slipped it in her pocket.

Just the Facts

Joanna Elizabeth Troutman was born on February 19, 1818 in Crawford County, Georgia. Her father was Hiram Baldwin Troutman, of Bibb County, Georgia. Her mother's name is not given in any of my sources. Joanna had three brothers: John, Marcellus, and Bainbridge. They lived on a 5,000-acre plantation on the Flint River, known as Elmwood because of elm groves surrounding the house. The house is no longer standing.

Joanna attended school at Scottsboro, Georgia, and at Barronsville, South Carolina.

In the evenings, she helped her father at his inn, the Troutman Inn, located in Knoxville, Georgia. The inn burned down in 1928 and a Presbyterian Church now stands there.

The accounts of how Joanna decided to make the Lone Star flag differ on the details. They agree that she used silk skirts to make the background and the star, and that she embroidered the motto "Liberty or Death" on one side, and the Latin motto *"Ubi Libertas Habitat Ibi Patria Est"*—where liberty dwells, there is my country—on the other. They also agree that she gave the completed flag to Lieutenant Colonel William Ward to carry to Lieutenant Hugh McLeod, and that McLeod sent her a letter thanking her for the flag.

However, one account says that after hearing of the troops marching to Texas, she was sitting on the porch at Elmwood with her family and saw the stars and decided that the North Star reminded her of Texas' lone fight for freedom. Then she went to the inn the next day and other girls in the town helped her make the flag.

Another account says that she met Hugh McLeod while she was working at the inn, and that McLeod gave her the idea of the star, and asked her to make the flag. She went home and her mother helped her plan materials to make the flag and the motto. Then she made it over the course of the next day or so, and took it to the inn to give it to McLeod.

I have used this second version because it seems most likely. The circumstances surrounding the idea and creation of the flag are not as important as the fact that she made the flag and that it was flown in front of the Georgia troops.

Joanna's flag was first flown in Texas at the American Hotel in Velasco on January 8, 1836. When they raised the flag, a ceremony was held and the following poem was composed and dedicated to Joanna. According to Henry David Pope's *A Lady and A Lone Star Flag* (1936), it was later published in the *Telegraph and Register*, printed at San Felipe de Austin.

The Flag Serves Texas

This silken banner! This silken banner,
In glorious triumph soon shall wave
O'er forest wide and green savannah
Borne by the chivalrous and brave.

Yes, it shall proudly float above
The heads of those whose hearts beat high
For deeds of fame, whose ardent love
Of freedom glows in every eye.

And now this banner is unfurled
By Georgia's sons in stranger lands.

Breathes there a man in this wide world
Could wrest it from a Georgian's hands?

No, no, 'twould be as vain to try
To snatch from him his banner bright
As 'twould be bid the sun on high
Cease to emit his glorious light.

For sooner would a Georgian die
And slumber in a soldier's grave
Than see this flag, when floating high
struck to a despot's cringing slave.

Maiden, it ne'er shall be disgraced
By those to whom thou dost entrust
Its destiny, but be replaced
In that fair hand, bright as at first.

The Georgia troops carried the Lone Star flag with them as they went on to join with the troops at the Mission of La Bahia at Goliad. On March 8, 1836, the troops received word that Texas had declared itself free from Mexican rule. They raised the flag during the celebration that followed. At sunset, while lowering the flag, it snarled in the ropes and the banner tore. The tatters remained flying until Santa Anna had completed his mission of killing the American troops on March 27, 1836. No remnants of Joanna's flag survive today.

Joanna married Colonel Solomon Lewis Pope, a lawyer of Montgomery, Alabama, on her 21st birthday—February 19, 1839. They were married at sunrise in Crawford County by the Reverend Mr. Dickerson. Years later, Colonel Pope was forced to give up his law practice due to poor health, and he and Joanna moved to Elmwood. On that beautiful plantation, they had four children. Henry Bainbridge Pope was born

July 29, 1842. Marcellus Troutman Pope was born February 1, 1845 in Macon County, Tuskeegee, Alabama. John Solomon Pope was born November 12, 1847, in Floyd County, Georgia. Solomon Lewis Pope II was born May 12, 1852 in Floyd County, Georgia, and died in 1882 at the age of 30.

Joanna's husband, Solomon Pope, died at Elmwood on October 2, 1872 and was buried in the family plot on the plantation. Joanna married W. G. Vinson three years later, on December 23, 1875. W. G. Vinson was a member of the Georgia Legislature from Crawford County. They had no children.

A bronze statue marks Joanna Troutman's grave in Austin, Texas. Photo by Chris Bolté.

Four years later, Joanna died at Elmwood at 10:00 a.m. on July 23, 1879. She was buried alongside her first husband and her sons at Elmwood. Her remains rested there until 1913, when the state of Texas moved her, with her relatives' permission, to the State Cemetery in Austin, Texas. In his message to the Texas Senate and House of Representatives, Governor O. B. Colquitt called Joanna "the 'Betsy Ross' of the Republic of Texas." Six years later, a famous Texas sculptor named Pompeo Coppini created a bronze statue in honor of Joanna. The statue shows Joanna apparently finishing the last stitch of the flag.

Check It Out!

Coulter, E. Merton. *Georgia: A Short History*. 306-307. North Carolina: University of North Carolina Press, 1947.

Knight, Lucian Lamar. *Georgia's Landmarks, Memorials and Legends*. 34-38. Volume 1. Atlanta: The Byrd Printing Company, 1913.

Maguire, Jack. "Who Was the Betsy Ross of Texas?" *Texas Highway*. May 1986. 10-11. [copy provided by the Texas Woman's University Library]

Pope, Henry David. *A Lady and A Lone Star Flag: The Story of Joanna Troutman*. San Antonio: The Naylor Company, 1936. [Autographed copy held by the University of Mississippi Library.]

Vinson, Edward R. "Texas' Betsy Ross and the Men of Goliad." *Texas Celebrates! The First 150 Years*. 113-117. A special publication. Dallas: Southwest Media Corp., 1985.

Online Resources

For more information on the complete history of Joanna's efforts, go to *www.flash.net/~alamo3/republic/flags/troutmanflag.html.*

To learn about Texas history, go to *www.rootsweb.com/~txvalver/texas.html.*

Wait 'Til You See This!

The bronze statue marking Joanna Troutman's grave is easily visible when you enter the State Cemetery in Austin. The monument also commemorates the men who died at Goliad.

A silver spoon and fork from Santa Anna's private collection, given to Joanna by Sam Houston after Santa Anna's defeat, are on display in the Witte Museum in San Antonio.

Joanna's portrait hangs at the state Capitol in Austin, Texas.

A plaque set in white stone stands on the lawn of the Knoxville, Georgia court house. In part the plaque says, "On this site in 1835, Joanna Troutman gave to a company of Georgia soldiers…a 'Lone Star' Flag, which she had made…."

Other Sources

Blashfield, Jean F. *Awesome Almanac of Texas.* 10,181. Walworth: B&B Publishing, 1995.

Westbury, Elaine. Copy of manuscript from Knoxville, Georgia court house library, entitled "Joanna Troutman." Undated.

"Georgia Girl Made Texas Flag." Copy of manuscript from Knoxville, Georgia court house library. No date or author given.

"Joanna Troutman." *Handbook of Texas*. 804, Volume 2.

Sherr, Lynn and Jurate Kazickas. *Susan B. Anthony Slept Here: A Guide to American Women's Landmarks*. 429. New York: Random House, 1994.

Annie Ellsworth

1843

Historic First Words

Annie sipped fresh orange juice and wondered what the day would hold. Every day in Washington, D.C. was filled with new people and exciting happenings. She wondered about the bill her father had been pushing through Congress the night before, March 3, on behalf of their friend Samuel Morse. Her father, Henry Ellsworth, as the first U.S. Commissioner of Patents, had an important job. She hoped, for her father's and Mr. Morse's sakes, the bill designed to pay for the installation and use of a new invention—the telegraph machine—had passed.

Footsteps in the hall announced her father's arrival for breakfast. He looked a little tired this morning, but only someone close to him would have noticed. Annie admired his stern features, knowing that beneath them lay a man with a loving heart.

"Good morning, Father," Annie said. "Did the bill pass?"

"Yes, it did," Henry said, sitting down at the head of the table. "I saw President Tyler sign it into law just before they broke up at midnight."

"Wonderful!" Annie cried. "May I congratulate Mr. Morse in person?"

Henry swallowed his bite of poached eggs and ham, and nodded. "Yes, dear."

"Thank you, Father."

Annie Ellsworth at 17 years old. Courtesy of Tippecanoe County Historical Assoc., Lafayette, Indiana.

Annie left the table and hurried to her room. She checked her hair in the mirror, noticing briefly her slender neck, dark eyes, and small nose and mouth. Then she picked up her shawl and gloves. She quickly went down the stairs and out the front door. She walked the few blocks to Samuel Morse's hotel. The front of the building stood regally along the street of the Capitol, its doorman keeping watch over the carved door. As Annie approached, the elaborately uniformed man pulled open the door and tipped his hat to her. His gesture made her feel older than 17, and she smiled at him.

"Good day, Miss," he said.

"Good day," Annie replied. She stood a moment in the large lobby. Several sofas were arranged to encourage conversation, with a few potted trees providing a hint of privacy. She crossed the marble floor to the front desk. She carried herself tall and proud, knowing she was the daughter of the very first Commissioner of Patents, appointed by the president himself.

"May I help you, Miss?" the concierge asked.

"I wish to speak to Mr. Samuel Morse," Annie said. "My name is Annie Ellsworth."

"Certainly. Bell boy! Take Miss Ellsworth to the parlor to see Mr. Morse."

The bell boy led her to the parlor to wait for Mr. Morse to arrive. The public room was comfortable and well-furnished.

A servant appeared and informed her that Mr. Morse had just gone into the breakfast room, and he would retrieve him. He bowed and left. She could hear the servant down the hall announcing her: "Sir, there is a young lady waiting to speak with you."

As she waited, she could barely contain her happiness for the final success Mr. Morse had achieved. She knew he had risked everything—his money, his reputation, his pride—to build the world's first telegraph from Washington to Baltimore. His work meant everything to him. And finally Congress would allow him to build it.

Mr. Morse soon emerged from the breakfast room and approached her. She smiled broadly at him.

"Why, Annie, what a pleasant surprise to see you so early this morning," Mr. Morse said, crossing the room.

"I have come to congratulate you."

"Indeed, for what?"

"On the passage of your bill," Annie said.

"Oh! No, my young friend, you are mistaken; I was in the Senate chamber till after the lamps were lighted, and my senatorial friends assured me there was no chance for me."

"But," Annie replied with a smile, "it is you that are mistaken. Father was there at the adjournment at midnight, and saw the President put his name to your bill, and I asked father if I might come and tell you, and he gave me leave. Am I the first to tell you?"

Mr. Morse's mouth opened, but no words came out.

"Yes, Annie," he said finally, "you are the first to inform me, and now I am going to make you a promise; the first dispatch on the completed line from Washington to Baltimore shall be yours."

"Well," Annie said, "I shall hold you to your promise."

Annie went home after chatting a few minutes with Mr. Morse. She was so happy for him, and to be the first to tell him of his good fortune, and then to be given the privilege of choosing the first words. It had been a remarkable morning.

Little more than a year later, Morse completed the telegraph line from Washington to Baltimore. A group of important men gathered around a table in Washington in the Supreme Court Chambers to watch the historic event. Annie stood quietly, and a bit nervously, among the other guests taking part in this special day. She saw Henry Clay who was running for president, and Dolly Madison, the wife of James Madison, fourth president of the United States. Annie noticed that some of the people were smiling, others looked like they doubted it would work at all.

Mr. Morse took his seat and turned to Annie. "What will the first message be, Annie?"

She handed him a piece of paper. On it were the words "What hath God wrought!", a quote from the Bible. He smiled his approval and turned to the machine in front of him. He quickly tapped out the message using the key lever and the dot-and-dash alphabet he created, which would be called Morse Code.

The crowd waited silently. The message traveled 40 miles through the cable strung on poles all the way to the B&O railroad station in Baltimore, Maryland. Then it was decoded and sent back to them via the same wires. When the telegraph machine in front of Samuel began tapping out his message a few minutes later, the room erupted in yells and hollers. It had worked! The new era of the telegraph had arrived.

Annie grinned. Samuel stood and handed her the original message. She held it tightly, sure she would treasure it—and this moment—for her lifetime.

Just the Facts

Ann Ellsworth was born January 6, 1827 in New Haven, Connecticut.

Her father was Henry Leavitt Ellsworth. He was born at Windsor, Connecticut on November 10, 1791. Henry graduated from Yale College in 1810, and was a classmate of Samuel Morse. He went on to study law at the Law School in Litchfield, Connecticut. He was appointed commissioner to the Indian tribes of the Far West, and then commissioner of the Patent Office in 1836. Henry died December 27, 1858 in Fair Haven, Connecticut, and was buried at New Haven, Connecticut.

Annie's mother, Nancy Allen Goodrich Ellsworth, was born in 1793. She died January 14, 1847 and is buried at Greenbush cemetery in West Lafayette, Indiana.

Annie had two brothers, Edward A., who died October 13, 1837 at the age of 21, and Henry W. Ellsworth who was born in 1814 at Windsor, Connecticut. Henry W. graduated from Yale University in 1834 and later became one of the first authors of Tippecanoe County, Indiana, when he wrote *Valley of the Upper Wabash, Indiana.*

When Ann was 17 years old, her father's friend, Samuel Finley Breeze Morse, was waiting for final approval by Congress to build the world's first telegraph line from Washington, D.C. to Baltimore, Maryland. Samuel had given up on its passage before the Congress adjourned at midnight, and returned to his hotel. Henry Ellsworth, then the first U.S. Commissioner of Patents, managed to get the bill voted on and passed by a vote of 89 to 83 on March 3, 1843. Henry told Ann the next morning and she was given permission to congratulate Morse, and became the first person to tell him the good news. For this, he promised to let her choose the first words, which she did with her mother's help. She chose the Bible verse Numbers 23:23, "What hath God wrought!"

A little more than a year later—March 24, 1844—the message was sent via Morse's telegraph to Baltimore and back in a matter of moments. Because Annie had written the message and delivered it to Morse, she has been honored as the first telegraph messenger girl.

Annie lived in Washington for another year, then her family moved to Lafayette, Indiana in 1845. Her father became one of the largest landowners in the area. He sent for a young lawyer he knew to help with the management of his property. The man's name was Roswell C. Smith. He lived in Stockton House, on the northwest corner of South and Seventh streets, with the Ellsworths. (This house was torn down August 29, 1956.) He and Annie were married on July 5, 1857 at the family home. They had two daughters. They built their own home, which they called Cedar Cottage, a block south of the family home, on the northwest corner of Seventh and Columbia streets. The house has since been torn down.

In 1870 the Smiths moved to New York City, where Roswell started publishing magazines, notably *St. Nicholas, Scribner's* and *Century.* They lived at 145 West 58th Street, in an apartment house. After suffering many illnesses, Roswell died on April 19, 1892 at the age of 63.

According to her death certificate, Annie died at 1:00 a.m. on January 21, 1900 from kidney failure ("chronic nephritis—uraenemia"), at her home in New York at the age of 73 years 15 days. She was buried at Mount Clare Cemetery in New York on January 24 at 9 a.m.

Check It Out!

Quackenbush, Robert. *Quick, Annie, Give Me a Catchy Line.* 1983.

Morse, Edward Lind, ed. *Samuel F. B. Morse: His Letters and Journals.* 198-203, 222-25. Volume II. Kennedy Galleries, Inc. New York: Da Capo Press, 1973.

Coe, Lewis. *The Telegraph: A History of Morse's Invention and Its Predecessors in the United States.* 32. Jefferson: McFarland & Co., Inc. Publishers, 1993.

Mabee, Carleton. *The American Leonardo: A Life of Samuel F. B. Morse.* 259-261, 274-277. 1943. New York: Octagon Books, Division of Farrar, Straus & Giroux, Inc., 1969.

More information can be obtained from the Tippecanoe County Historical Association, 909 South Street, Lafayette, IN 47901-1414, (765) 742-8411.

Online Resources

The paper strip containing the original telegraph message sent by Morse is held by the Library of Congress. You can view the four segments at *http://lcweb.loc.gov/exhibits/treasures/trupscale/ res/drill_res_026.html.*

Wait 'Til You See This!

The Tippecanoe County Museum (1001 South Street, Lafayette, IN 47901) has a bust of Annie as a woman, on the second floor in the "Portraits from the Past" exhibit. You can call (765) 476-8411 for information and hours.

In May 1944, the U.S. Postal Service commemorated the centennial of the invention of the telegraph by issuing a 3¢ postage stamp with the words "What Hath God Wrought!" upon it.

The duplicate of the message sent by Morse is on display at the Connecticut historical rooms at Hartford, Connecticut.

A government building on the east side of Seventh Street NW, between E and F Streets, in Washington, D.C., is the site where the first telegraph office stood. A bronze tablet was placed here in 1913 that notes that Morse operated the first public telegraph office in the building. The tablet includes the text of Annie's message.

The house where Annie lived used to stand at 806 South Street, on the corner of Seventh and South Streets, West Lafayette, Indiana.

Other Sources

Baker, Mrs. Otto C. "Resident Helps Farming" and "The Ellsworth Family." *The Journal and Courier.* West Lafayette: December 3, 1955 and December 10, 1955. Second and third in a series of three articles on Henry Leavitt Ellsworth.

Harris, John M. "What hath God wrought?" Copy of article obtained from files at Tippecanoe County Historical Association.

Heimlich, Herbert H. "A 17-Year-Old Girl Suggested the First Telegraph Message, Which was Received in Baltimore 100 Years Ago." Manuscript for article. West Lafayette: 1944.

Heimlich, Herbert H. Untitled. Manuscript for article about new three-cent stamp. West Lafayette: 1944.

Martin, Fern Honeywell, and Paula Alexander Woods. *Greater Lafayette, A Pictorial History*. 42. St. Louis: G. Bradley Pubs., Inc., 1989.

PR Newswire. "Morse Bicentennial Marked by Re-Enactment of Historic Telegraph Transmission." PR Newswire Association, Inc., May 23, 1991, Domestic News Section.

Proctor, John Clagett. "Morse Established His First Telegraph Office in Washington." *The Sunday Star*. Washington, D.C.: February 10, 1929.

Proctor, John Clagett. "Another Landmark of Capital Passes." *The Sunday Star*. Washington, D.C.: September 14, 1930.

Salmagundi. Editorial. *The Baltimore Sun*. May 24, 1994, 12A.

Seders, Debbie. "First Telegraphic Message Part of Lafayette's History." *Journal and Courier*. Friday, June 27, 1975, C10.

Sherr, Lynn and Jurate Kazickas. *Susan B. Anthony Slept Here: A Guide to American Women's Landmarks*. 140. New York: Random House, 1994.

VIRGINIA REED

1846-47

Surviving the Pioneer Adventure

Virginia heard the call of the wagon master. Time for the wagon train to continue west. She swung up onto her pony, Billy, and rode alongside her father, James Reed. Wagons lurched into motion, each pulled by three or four pair of oxen. The wagons contained everything the families needed to start a new life in the territory of California. Virginia's family had packed enough supplies to last for the six month journey.

"Come on, Virginia," Papa said. "Let's ride ahead and find a good camp site for this evening."

As Billy trotted steadily along, Virginia inhaled the fragrance of wild flowers growing everywhere on the plains of Kansas. She was glad to have her pony, so she didn't have to ride in a slow, bouncy wagon. Her family had three wagons, one of which was built for Grandma Keyes' comfort. However, Virginia enjoyed riding her pony. That was the one great pleasure she had looked forward to when her father decided the family would move from Springfield, Illinois, to California. After a year of preparations, they were on the trail west.

The group of people that had gathered to head west numbered 31. There were Virginia's mother and father, Grandma Keyes, sister Patty, brothers James Jr. and Thomas, as well as a household helper named Eliza Williams and her brother, Baylis. The Reeds had also brought along three men to drive the oxen. Two other families had decided to join with the Reeds on the trek: George and Tamsen Donner and their five children, along with Jacob Donner (George's brother) and his wife, Elizabeth, and their seven children.

Each morning Virginia and her father would ride ahead to locate a camp site, and then rejoin the party to lead them there. Her mother and siblings rode in the wagon with Grandma, who was ill but seemed to be feeling better as they jolted along. To 12-year-old Virginia, the entire trip was a great adventure. She was glad that her seven-year-old sister, Patty, had taken it upon herself to sit and entertain Grandma during the trip.

On Tuesday, May 19, 1846, they reached the Caw River in Kansas. They had been traveling the trail since April 14 and everything was going smoothly. To cross the river, they needed to use the ferry, which was run by Caw Indians. Virginia kept a close eye on the Indians, certain they would try to sink the boat midstream. She remembered Grandma's stories about being mistreated and kept captive when she was a child.

There were two boats, each able to carry two wagons at a time across the river. Virginia watched as each wagon was pulled as close as possible to the river by the oxen. Then the oxen were unhitched and the men lifted and pushed the fully-loaded wagon onto the ferry. Then the people would join the wagon. When the ferry was ready, the Caws used long poles to steer the boat across the river. The oxen and horses were forced to swim across. Virginia let out a deep sigh when they crossed the river without incident.

Camping that night at Soldier Creek, they found they had caught up with another wagon train, known as the Bryant Party. Virginia had never seen so many wagons in one place. She gazed at the hundreds of people, dogs, horses, and oxen. The air vibrated with the smell of meals being cooked over open fires, and the sounds of dogs barking, men shouting, and children laughing.

The next morning they continued their journey west, some people walking, others riding in wagons or on horseback. Days passed, one very much like another. On Tuesday, May 26, the wagon train reached the Big Blue river, where the party was forced to stop. The river was 20 feet above normal due to recent rains upstream. They made camp and the men began making rafts to carry the wagons and people across the rapid river.

"Virginia, I think Grandma is getting worse," Patty said one evening.

"What do you mean?" Virginia asked, looking at her sister's dark, troubled eyes. She knew her grandma wasn't well, but they had hoped she would make it to California.

"She's not eating, and she can't talk," Patty said.

Virginia went to bed that night wondering how her grandma would survive the tough trails ahead. Virginia lay listening to the owls hooting somewhere in the distance, and the dying cooking fires popping outside. Mostly, though, she listened to her grandma's labored breathing. After a long time, she drifted off to sleep.

When Virginia awoke, she looked at her grandma's bed and it was empty. Where was she? She tossed back the covers and jumped out of bed.

"Ma! Where's Grandma?" she asked, climbing out of the wagon into bright sunshine.

"Shh, hon, come here," her mother said. Tears glistened in her eyes as she pulled Virginia to her. Virginia knew her grandma had died. Her own tears cascaded down her cheeks as she clutched Ma's waist.

For the first time on the trip, everyone stopped working that day building rafts. Instead, they cut down a cottonwood tree and built a coffin. Someone found a large grey stone and carved "Sarah Keyes; born in Virginia" on it. At 2:00 p.m. everyone gathered under an oak tree. Reverend J. A. Cornwall said a few words of comfort as the coffin was lowered into the ground and covered with dirt. Virginia and Patty joined in planting flowers on the grave. Virginia's tears fell on the fresh earth as she patted the wildflowers in place. When that task was finished, there was nothing more to do except mourn.

The next day, however, work resumed as normal. Once the rafts were completed and everyone safely across, the group continued their journey through rough, forested country until they reached the Platte River. A valley stretched before them, deep green, with many different kinds of wildflowers growing, and a wide, shallow river flowing down the center. Virginia kicked her pony to gallop across the plain, stopping occasionally to dismount and pick some of the colorful flowers. They reminded her of Grandma.

Traveling between 15 and 20 miles a day along the river, they passed Court House Rock, Chimney Rock, and Scott's Bluff. When they stopped for the night, the 40 wagons pulled into a circle, with the livestock corralled in the center to graze. Virginia watched Eliza as she set up the cooking fire and struggled to prepare the meal. Virginia's stomach rumbled. So much exercise in a day left her drooling for her nightly buffalo or antelope steak.

Virginia helped Eliza prepare a wonderful dinner to celebrate the Fourth of July at Fort Laramie. After the feast, several Sioux approached Papa, carrying buffalo robes, buckskin, moccasins, and grass ropes. Virginia watched their eyes light on Billy, seeing his strong legs and fine coat. The Sioux dropped their articles beside several of their own horses. They wanted Billy in trade. Virginia gasped. Papa smiled and shook his head at the Sioux. A frown appeared on the warrior's face, then he added several more ponies to the trade. Virginia looked at Papa, as he shook his head again. Finally, the Sioux offered an old coat with brass buttons, hoping that would sway the deal. Papa shook his head yet again. She smiled and ran to throw her arms around her pony's neck. Billy was safe.

Two days later the wagon train moved on. The Sioux moved on also. There were so many Sioux that it took several days to pass the caravan of wagons. They swarmed around the large wagon that Virginia's grandma had ridden in, fascinated by a large mirror and by the stove pipe sticking out of the canvas roof. Virginia could tell the Sioux still wanted to buy Billy, but he wasn't for sale.

"Virginia, these Sioux want Billy," Papa said, riding up alongside Virginia.

"They know a good pony when they see one," Virginia said, smiling with pride.

"I want you to ride in the wagon for a while."

"No! I want to ride Billy," Virginia said. "I'm fine. I can handle him, even with all the Sioux around."

"I'd feel better if you were safely in the wagon. Milt will take care of him."

Reluctantly, Virginia dismounted and climbed into the wagon. Angry, she decided to see just how long the line of Sioux was, and thus how long she'd have to ride in the wagon. She grabbed a small, collapsible telescope from a rack and pulled it open with a loud click. The sound startled the Sioux warriors crowded around the wagon. They turned their horses and galloped away. Virginia laughed.

"Mother, I could fight the whole Sioux tribe with a spyglass!" she said.

A few days later, Virginia was riding Billy again. She noticed that her pony was having trouble keeping up with the oxen. She motioned to her father, who rode over to her.

"Papa, Billy seems tired."

"This has been a tough trip for him," Papa said. He hesitated, then added, "If he can't keep up, we'll have to leave him behind."

"I could never leave him! Out here in the middle of nowhere? Who would care for him?" Tears trickled down her cheeks as she thought about abandoning her best friend in the middle of the prairie. After all they had been through, growing up together, and now this adventure into the west, defending him from the Sioux's attempts to buy him. Leave him? Never.

As the day wore on, Virginia slowly realized that Billy could not complete the trip. The constant travel had become too much for him. He stopped, unable to go any farther. Tears leaked from her eyes and she muffled a sob. Her father had Milt stop the oxen. She dismounted from her friend and removed the bridle and saddle, crying uncontrollably. Then she climbed into the back of the wagon, and sat where she could watch Billy grow smaller and finally disappear as the oxen pulled the wagon toward the sunset. She cried all night until she had no more tears to cry.

The trek seemed endless. No longer did she have her Grandma's gentle ways and engaging stories. Billy had been left behind, alone. Surely, the trip could not get worse. Riding in the wagon proved harder than riding on horseback, because of the rocking and jolting of the hard wheels over bumps and rocks. She wished they had already traveled the 2,000 miles from Missouri to the west coast.

After a lengthy debate among all the adults, one group of emigrants, including Virginia's family, decided to take a shortcut over the Sierra mountains—a new route that was claimed to be better and faster than the usual route. Virginia hoped so.

On July 31, the group taking the shortcut, known as Hasting's Cut-off, peeled off from the larger group. In all, 87 people searched for a faster way. A few days along the new trail, though, they realized that they'd been lied to. They struggled through rocky canyons where the trail disappeared. The men cut the heavy underbrush away and made a road bed with the branches. At one point, they reached the end of a canyon and were forced to double team the oxen to pull the wagons up the steep hill. When they reached the shore of the Great Salt Lake in Utah, everyone, including the animals, were exhausted. Ahead of them lay what they'd been told was 40 miles of desert to cross.

Virginia helped prepare for the crossing by filling many water vessels so they'd have enough water for themselves, the oxen, and horses. That evening they started across the barren land. Virginia knew that by traveling at night the walk would be cooler and they'd retain more of the water they drank. The next morning they kept walking, all through the long, hot day, and again all night. As darkness began to fall on the third night, Virginia looked ahead and saw nothing but more of the same vast, empty land. She heard her father give orders to his drivers on how to handle the oxen, then he rode ahead on his horse to find water. After he left, Virginia saw one of the weaker oxen fall to the ground. Milt, along with the other two drivers, quickly unhitched the oxen and drove them ahead to water.

Virginia and her family stayed with the wagon to wait until they brought the animals back. The wagons contained all their food and water; all their supplies to survive the winter once they reached California.

If they reached California.

Virginia wished her father would return soon. Her mother had one of her bad headaches. Her family hoped that, even though her mother had been ill before, she would feel better when they reached California. Waiting by the wagon all night, wondering where her father was, and when the drivers would return with the oxen, Virginia could only pray that they would hurry.

As the sun rose, Papa rode up to the wagon. Virginia ran and threw her arms around him. She was so happy to see him, and so thirsty! The water barrels were almost empty.

"We'll have to wait for the drivers to return," he said. "They shouldn't be too long. I passed them on my way back."

They sat in the shade of the wagon and watched for the men. When night began to fall, Papa stood and said, "We must try to reach some of the other wagons. Something must have happened to the drivers."

Virginia walked beside Patty, hour after hour, struggling to put one foot in front of the other. Her mouth burned with thirst. All she could think about was water. She fought to take another step, then another. Surely the trip couldn't become any worse.

Virginia lifted her weary head at the sound of something rushing toward her in the darkness. The whole family stopped to listen.

"What is it?" Patty whispered.

"Shh," Virginia whispered back.

Their five dogs started barking. Virginia could hear her favorite, Cash, adding his unique voice to those of Tyler, Barney, Trailer, and Tracker. Papa gathered everyone behind him, picking up little Thomas as he drew his gun. Out of the inky stillness came a young steer, crazy with the need for a drink. The steer ran right at the group, finally turning when the dogs charged it and scared it away. Virginia was no longer tired, only scared. Patty clutched her hand.

"Let's keep going," Papa said.

Ten miles of walking across the desert in the dark brought them to Jacob Donner's wagon. Everyone in the wagon was asleep. Virginia and Patty did as their father told them and laid down under the wagon to sleep. Virginia huddled against Patty, trying to keep her warm from the wind that chilled them.

"Papa, I'm cold," Patty said.

"Me, too," Virginia said.

Papa called the dogs and soon had them snuggled around the children under the wagon. Cash lay close by, his nose near Virginia's hand. She was glad of his company.

When the sun peeked over the horizon, Papa left to find out what had happened to his oxen. He came back with bad news—all of them were lost. Virginia feared they would never make it to California. Obviously, they had to keep moving, they couldn't stay here on the edge of the desert forever. A week passed while Papa and the other men in the party searched for the oxen. The loss of the 18 head of oxen meant the family was in trouble. Virginia heard Papa tell Mama that they would have to abandon two of the three wagons, and the third would be pulled by two yoke of borrowed oxen. They took the lightest wagon, leaving behind the specially-equipped one that rode most comfortably. Their family's belongings were divided among other wagons in the party. After checking their supplies, the party now knew they didn't have enough food to get them to California. Two men were sent ahead to Sutter's Fort for more supplies.

The rest of the party continued wearily on. Virginia noticed the men were short-tempered and harsh. Then, on October 5, 1846, those hard feelings erupted into a fight. Virginia wasn't able to see the fight, but soon found its consequences. While driving the oxen up a hill, Papa's wagon, driven by Milt, tangled with the Graves' wagon, driven by John Snyder. When the fight ended, Snyder lay dying on the ground with a knife wound from Papa's knife. The group was furious at James Reed. Virginia dressed Papa's wound, as Mama was slightly hurt during the scuffle. She washed off the blood, clipped back the hair from around the cut on his head, then applied a clean bandage. She felt proud of her ability to care for Papa. The party voted, and banished James Reed. He would be sent off alone, without a horse, a gun, or food and water. Virginia cried at the thought of her beloved Papa being left all alone.

"I can't leave you," Papa said to Mama.

"You may have to in order to save your own life," Mama replied. "And to bring supplies for the rest of us. Would you rather stay and watch our children starve? Or leave and bring back help?"

Papa was silent for a few moments, looking at each of his children, then Mama. Finally he nodded. "All right, I'll go. But the party has to promise to take care of you."

Without much fanfare, he headed out of camp, walking west along the trail the others would follow in the morning. As night fell, Virginia gathered Papa's rifle, pistol, ammunition, and food. Then she talked Milt into going with her to find Papa, to give him the supplies and his horse, Glaucus. What she didn't tell Milt was that she was going to ask Papa to take her with him.

They caught up with Papa and handed over the goods. Virginia threw her arms around his neck and said, "Papa, let me stay with you. Please, I want to go with you. I can help you."

"No, my little one. You must stay with Mama. It is impossible for you to go with me." He pried Virginia's arms from around his neck and gently pushed her toward Milt. "Take her back to camp. Keep her safe."

"Yes, sir." Milt turned to Virginia. "Let's get going. It's a good walk back."

Virginia cried all the way, afraid she'd never see Papa again. She cried so hard she could hardly walk. Finally they made it back to camp.

"Virginia! Where have you been?" Mama cried. "How could you run off like that? And Milt, how could you let her?"

Virginia saw tear tracks in the dust on her mother's face. This trip had been very hard for her mother. Virginia's siblings clutched her mother's long skirts. She had no husband to help calm her children's fears, or her own.

"I'm sorry, Mama."

"Go on and get some rest," Mama urged.

Virginia realized she must help her mother all she could while her father was away. She squared her shoulders and made up her mind to be strong.

The next days were difficult for everyone. No one talked much. Everyone worried about the snowcapped mountains ahead of them that they had to cross. Would they make it over them before winter truly set in?

One day, Virginia's mother was told that her wagon would have to be abandoned, as it was too heavy and too much of a burden for the party. So, their belongings again were divided among the other wagons. Virginia's younger brothers rode on exhausted horses while everyone else trudged slowly beside the wagons. Virginia walked beside little Tommy to help keep him on the horse.

At last, on October 19, Charles Stanton, one of the men sent for food, returned with seven loaded mules. He also brought two Indian vaqueros (cowboys), Luis and Salvador. And news that Papa was alive!

Virginia helped load one mule with her family's belongings. She thought about all of the books, furniture, medicines, and valuables they had left Missouri with, and now they could pack everything they owned on one mule.

Virginia's mama mounted a mule, putting Tommy in her lap. Patty and Jim rode another mule, and Virginia rode behind Charles Stanton. They set off in the pouring rain, soaked to the skin. They headed toward the high mountains where the rain became snow that covered all the trails and roads. The wagons could not be dragged through the deep snow no matter how hard each family tried.

Stanton rode ahead to find the trail and came back saying they'd have to keep going until they reached the summit of the mountain. His idea of going on met with complaints of exhaustion and pleas to rest. The emigrants had started a large dead pine tree burning brightly. Reluctant to leave its warmth, they stayed.

That night it snowed. As Virginia lay wrapped in a blanket on the snow, every few minutes Mama shook the shawl that covered them to toss off the powdery flakes. With dawn came the realization that the snow was too deep and everyone too exhausted to fight their way through. They built three double cabins on the shore of what is now Donner Lake. The cabins were small, with openings for doors, but no windows, and flat roofs made from laying poles across from wall to wall, and then covering them with canvas, tents, hides, or whatever they could find to keep snow and rain out. They killed all the cattle and placed the meat in the snow to keep. At night, Virginia, her brothers, and her sister cuddled with the dogs for warmth.

Months passed and Christmas drew near. Virginia's stomach constantly gnawed with hunger. All the food was gone. She hated the stewed oxhide they ate, a nasty paste that kept them alive and little more. The men were so weak they could barely cut wood to make fires. Some mornings the snow had to be cleared out of the fireplace before a fire could be lit. Storms lasted for 10 days at a time, with the snow piling deeper outside until the snow buried the cabin. To start a fire, chips of wood were taken from the cabin itself.

Children cried, and the mothers cried with them as they watched their children starve. Virginia thought about bread occasionally, but not very often. Survival was the only thought. She was thankful for Patrick Breen, a kind, generous, Catholic man who had claimed the cabin as his for his family and allowed the Reeds to stay with him. He spent his days writing in his journal, reading from the Bible, and praying to God to help them find a way out.

They marked the passage of weeks by prayers on Sundays. At one point, Virginia promised God that she would become a Catholic like Mr. Breen, if He would spare them.

Christmas was a day like any other: they ate oxhide soup and said their prayers. Margaret Reed, however, had a surprise for the children at dinnertime. She had kept a few dried apples, a cup of white beans, one-half cup of rice, a small amount of tripe (ox stomach), and a small square piece of bacon to boil together for a soup.

"Mama! How wonderful. A Christmas dinner!" Virginia cried.

Tommy, Jimmy, and Patty laughed and clapped their hands with excitement. The smiles on their faces said more than words.

"Children, eat slowly, for this one day you can have all you wish," Margaret Reed said.

As the new year started, Margaret Reed could no longer stand by and watch her children die. They had already been forced to eat Cash, Virginia's favorite dog. They had eaten everything of the dog, making the meat last one week. Virginia packed a few items to take on their attempt to leave the Sierras. The escape party included Margaret Reed, Eliza, Milt Elliott, and Virginia.

Virginia worried that she wouldn't have the strength for the trip, but she knew she would try her hardest. If they could get over the mountain they could send supplies to those starving in the cabins. Once the younger children's cries quieted and they were left with the Breen family to be cared for, the group headed out. Virginia looked up to see the sun high in the sky and knew it was noon on this fourth day of January. They had no compass and only an idea of where to find the trail.

Milt led, wearing snowshoes to break a path for those behind. Before they'd gone very far, Eliza had to turn back, unable to manage the deep snow and bitter cold. Virginia walked, and sometimes crawled, climbing one steep, high mountain after another, only to find more lay ahead.

The first night they lit a fire and huddled around it, listening to the screams of animals in the surrounding forest. Virginia scanned the edge of the fire's glow, trying to see beyond it into the darkness. The wind moaned through the pine trees as if in sympathy with the tired, sore, and desperate travelers.

One morning when they awoke, they found that their night fire had melted a well in the snow, leaving them at the bottom of a deep pit.

"How do we get out without causing the snow to cave in on us?" Virginia asked. She rubbed an icy foot, trying to warm it.

Milt thought awhile, then started carving steps up the side. Once free from the well, Virginia told her mother about her foot being numb. When her mother looked at it, she shook her head.

"We'll have to go back. Her foot is frozen. We must warm it." She looked up to the summit of the mountain they were trying to climb. "I guess it's not to be."

Virginia limped behind the others, striving to keep up as best she could. Turning back was the same as failure to her, and it broke her heart that they were to be trapped once more. She knew she had no other choice, her feet hurt and she was so very cold. If only Milt could carry her for awhile, as he had on the way out, then maybe her feet could recover. But she knew that he was too weak to carry her at all. She was relieved when they finally reached the warmth of the cabin after being out in the snow for five days.

That night another storm whipped through the little valley by the lake. The wind and snow swirled and danced outside. Virginia realized they would have died had they been out on the mountain in such weather. She thanked God for her frozen foot.

Another month passed in the cold, snowbound cabin, eating oxhide soup and hanging on to life by willpower. Virginia's books, including her favorite *The Life of Daniel Boone*, had been burned and their leather covers eaten. On February 9, Milt Elliot died from starvation. Virginia cried at the loss of her "brother." Even though he'd been an employee, he was more like family. He had called Margaret Reed "Ma." Virginia and her mother carried Milt's body outside and buried it in the snow. As Virginia patted the snow over Milt's face, she cried harder.

Finally, on February 19, 1847, help arrived at the lake cabins. Patrick Breen heard shouts outside the cabin that evening, and when he poked his head out, he saw seven men loaded down with food and supplies.

"Relief, thank God, relief!" he cried.

A few days later, on February 22, a group of 23 men, women and children, including Virginia and her family, began the walk out of the mountains underneath a beautiful, sunny sky. Virginia was glad to be heading out of the snowbound camp, on her way to see Papa. Suddenly Patty and Tommy fell to the snow.

"Patty, come on. Get up," Virginia said. She tugged on Patty's hand, trying to help her stand.

"No, I can't. I can't go on," Patty said.

The rest of the party stopped to decide what to do. Mama stood beside her young children, without saying a word. Virginia could see tears in her eyes as she looked down the trail they were making.

"We'll all go back," Mama said. "I won't leave my children here."

Aquilla Glover flatly refused to let all of them go back. "Mrs. Reed, I will take them back to the cabin. You go on with the other two. These two have a better chance at the cabin than trying to walk out of here as worn out as they are."

"Mr. Glover, are you a Mason?" Mama asked. Virginia remembered that Papa was also a member of the Freemasons.

"Yes, Mrs. Reed, I am."

"Will you promise me on the word of a Mason that if we do not meet their father you will return and save my children?"

"I will, on my word as a Mason."

Even though Virginia knew it would be best for her younger siblings, she couldn't stop the tears as she hugged them farewell. Would she ever see them alive again? They were going back to eat oxhide soup and freeze in the cabins buried in snow. Virginia saw tears in some of the men's eyes before they turned away.

Patty looked up at her mother. "I want to see Papa, but I will take good care of Tommy, and I do not want you to come back."

"Darling, Patty. Be safe. Help is coming soon. Hold on," Mama said, kissing her daughter's forehead.

"If I do not see you again, Mother," Patty said, "do the best you can."

Patty and Tommy trudged behind Aquilla Glover and Sept Moutry as they led them back to the lake cabins to wait for the next relief party.

Virginia and the rest of the party kept walking, single file, through the deep snow. She was grateful for the men ahead of her breaking a trail with their snowshoes, but her weakened legs found it hard to walk. That night they slept on the snow. When they awoke at dawn, their clothing was frozen. They were up and moving before long, trying to travel as far as they could before the sun's light not only softened the snow, but blinded them as well.

Virginia saw her brother, Jimmy, struggle to step in a man's footprint, then place a knee on the crust between the man's steps and climb over to the next footprint. She could tell it was wearing him out. She was proud of her brother for the effort he was making to keep up with the group, and she motioned to her mother. Her mother's eyes rested briefly on the tiring boy.

"Come on, Jimmy, every step you take brings you closer to Papa," Mama said.

"I'm trying, Mama," Jimmy said.

During that day, one of the men couldn't walk any more, but he urged the party to go on without him. Virginia wondered if he'd survive until the next relief party arrived, or if he'd die waiting. They built him a fire and made a bed for him out of pine branches. He stretched out on the pine branches and smoked his pipe, content to stare at the flames.

"Can I stay with him?" Jimmy asked.

"Why would you want to do that?" Virginia asked, surprised. "Don't you want to see Papa?"

"But he looks so comfortable, and I could rest," Jimmy said.

"You must come with us, Jimmy," Virginia said, putting an arm around his shoulders. "We'll be out of here before long and we can get warm, and eat bread again. Come on, let's keep moving."

The party continued fighting their way through the snow until they reached where the rescue party had buried extra food for the return trip. The food pack was nothing but strips of cloth and paw prints. Virginia nearly cried when she realized they did not have enough food to make it off the mountain. She kept her tears to herself, however, and the group kept walking.

Virginia walked with her head down, concentrating on where she put her feet. She could tell they were about halfway down the western slope of the Sierra mountains. She grew weaker with each step, but she was determined to keep up with the group. Suddenly she heard a noise ahead and looked up. A group of men were approaching the party.

"Hello! Is Mrs. Reed with you? If she is, tell her Mr. Reed is here!" they called.

Virginia smiled and looked at Mama and saw her kneel down in the snow, suddenly weak from emotion. Virginia hurried as much as she could to see her father.

"Papa!" she cried, hugging him with the little strength she had left.

"Your mother, where is she?" he asked, hugging his daughter.

"She's just back there, in the snow." Virginia pointed to where her mother was recovering from her fainting spell.

"My darling Virginia," he said, his voice muffled against her hair. "And Jimmy! My big man. But where are Patty and Tommy?"

"They had to go back to the cabins. They were too weak and tired." Virginia let a tear slide down her face as she looked at her father. He handed Virginia a small bag of fresh bread he'd baked the night before. She inhaled its aroma, her mouth watering at the rich smell, then began handing out pieces to the anxious children gathering around her.

"I'll keep going then. I'll bring them out with me." After hugging his wife and encouraging her to hurry off the mountain, he left and disappeared up the trail.

Knowing they were close to safety, the group's spirits lifted and they found renewed energy to keep walking. Finally, they cleared the mountains and reached Sutter's Fort, where many of the suffering families found a place to stay and recover.

Virginia, her mother, and her brother were invited to stay at the Sinclair's house, and were treated kindly. They had hot food to eat, hot coffee to drink, and a warm fire to sit by. But Virginia couldn't relax with Papa, Patty, and Tommy still on the mountain.

Several days passed and the worry and tension in the cabin grew. Virginia feared the others on the mountain wouldn't make it out, especially since it was raining outside, which meant it was snowing on the mountain. Mama stood by the door, staring up at the mountain, waiting for them.

"I think—could it be? Yes! They're coming!" cried Mama.

Virginia rushed to the door, afraid it wasn't true. But it was! Her family had all survived the dreadful hunger, freezing temperatures, and desperation. The great adventure was finally over.

Just the Facts

Virginia Backenstoe was born in 1834. Her mother, Margaret, married James Reed sometime later after Virginia's father presumably died. James Reed adopted Virginia. James Reed was 42 at the time of the expedition to California in 1846. He was an Irish-born furniture maker from Springfield, Illinois. He died in 1874. Margaret was 32 years old, and suffered from migraine headaches that left her weak. She died in 1861.

Virginia had two stepbrothers, James (born in 1840) and Thomas (born in 1842), and one stepsister, Martha (born in 1837), who was called Patty.

VIRGINIA E. REED.
(Mrs. J. M. Murphy)
1880.

Virginia Reed Murphy, 1880. From Across the Plains in the Donner Party.

The idea to move to California initiated with Virginia's father. Neighbors Jacob and George Donner decided to join the Reeds on the journey west. The group became known as the Donner Party. They left Springfield, Illinois on April 14, 1846 with a total of 31 people in the wagon train. By the time they departed Ft. Bridger on July 31, 1846 there were 74 people and 19 wagons in the wagon train. The group that was snowed in at Donner lake consisted of 83 people. Of those, 42 died during the four months at the lakes. Only 18 of the original 31 people who left Springfield, Illinois reached California.

Virginia wrote a letter to her friend (or cousin) Mary, on May 16, 1847, in which she told about the hardships at the lake camp:

> *Oh, Mary I have wrote you half of the trouble we have had but I have wrote you enough to let you know that you don't know what trouble is. Thank the Good God we have all got through the only family that did not eat human flesh. We have left everything but I don't care for that—we got through.*

Many of the people starving at the camps died, and the survivors were forced to eat their dead comrades in order to stay alive. The Reeds were one of the families who did not have to resort to that desperate step.

Virginia refused a wedding proposal from Perry McCoon shortly after arriving at Johnson's Ranch in California. She went to school, then in 1850 married a Catholic named John M. Murphy. John had crossed the Sierras in 1844 with the Stephens-Murphy-Townsend Party. They settled in San Jose and had nine children.

Virginia and Patty both suffered from emotional scars throughout their lives, but they recovered physically in a short amount of time.

Patty married Frank Lewis in 1856 and they had eight children.

In May 1846, Virginia wrote her story about the Donner Party in a letter, which was published by the Illinois Journal in December 1846. Later, in 1891, she wrote another account "Across the Plains in the Donner

Party" for *Century Magazine*. This account is considered to be less accurate than the original, though her memories of key events are believable.

Check It Out!

Mullen, Frank Jr. *The Donner Party Chronicles: A Day-by-Day Account of a Doomed Wagon Train*. A Halycon Imprint of the Nevada Humanities Committee, 1997.

Murphy, Virginia Reed. *Across the Plains in the Donner Party*. Fairfield: Ye Galleon Press, 1998.

Stewart, George R., Jr. *Ordeal by Hunger: The Story of the Donner Party*. New York: Henry Holt & Co., 1936.

Sutton, Margaret. *Palace Wagon Family: A True Story of the Donner Party*. New York: Alfred A. Knopf, 1957.

Online Resources

There are many online sources you can turn to for information on the Donner Party. One very thorough web site, that links to other sites, is *http://members.aol.com/DanMRosen/donner*.

The Donner Memorial State Park has some information and many links to related sites. Go to *www.ceres.ca.gov/sierradsp/donner.html*.

Wait 'Til You See This!

Donner Memorial State Park is located in Sierra, Nevada where many of the emigrants died from starvation and illness. A large monument stands at the site of one of the cabins. The base of the monument is the same height as the snow that awful winter—22 feet deep.

The Emigrant Trail Museum is also at Donner Memorial State Park. A visit takes about one hour. Starting from the side of the museum is a self-guiding nature trail that is about a half mile loop. One- to two-hour hikes start each morning at 10:00 am. For more information, call 530-582-7892.

Other Sources

Barnard, Edward S., editor. *Story of the Great American West*. 163. Pleasantville: Reader's Digest Association, 1977.

Horn, Huston. *The Pioneers*. 85-119. New York: Time-Life Books, 1974.

Sherr, Lynn and Jurate Kazickas. *Susan B. Anthony Slept Here: A Guide to American Women's Landmarks*. 56. New York: Random House, 1994.

ABIGAIL GARDNER

1857

Surviving the Spirit Lake Massacre

Abbie set the steaming plate of pancakes on the wooden table. The cabin echoed with her family's chatter as they prepared to eat breakfast. Her father was preparing to make the 80 mile journey to the nearest town to buy supplies. Her younger brother, Rowland, added a log to the fire that crackled in the fireplace, warding off the cold from the winter's deep snow outside.

She watched older sister Mary pin back her one-year-old daughter Amanda's hair, while Mary's husband, Harvey, looked on. Little Albert, Mary's four-year-old son, darted about the room, his natural energy finding a release.

"Abbie, would you get the coffee pot, please?" Abbie's mother, Frances, asked.

Abbie retrieved the pot and poured coffee into the cups. Her mother set a crock of maple syrup on the table. As they started to take their seats, a knock sounded at the door.

"Who could that be?" Abbie's father Rowland asked. He opened the door and saw a Sioux brave, asking for breakfast.

"Of course," Rowland said, stepping back.

Abbie knew her parents both believed the Sioux were friendly and they should try to help each other all they could. She quickly added a place at the table for their guest. They sat down and began to eat. Before long, another knock, another Sioux. Then another and another. Abbie sensed something amiss when the leader of the band, Inkpaduta (meaning Scarlet Point), arrived. He looked to be about 50 years old, was six feet tall, and had marks on his face from having small pox. Abbie shuddered at his horrific appearance. Soon Inkpaduta, 14 warriors, their squaws, and papooses (babies) crowded into the cabin.

Abbie's father built this cabin. Photo by Steven Ohrn. Courtesy State Historical Society of Iowa.

The visitors made signs that they were friends, and wanted to trade. Abbie's parents gave them as much food as they could, hoping they would be satisfied and leave. Suddenly, one brave demanded ammunition for his gun. Abbie's father started to hand him a few guncaps when the brave grabbed the box from his hand. Abbie watched in growing alarm as another brave made a grab for the powder horn hanging against the wall. Harvey stepped in and didn't let him have the gunpowder. The brave grew angry and raised his gun to Harvey's head, but Harvey quickly grasped the barrel and yanked it away.

The door opened and two neighbors, Dr. Harriott and Mr. Snyder, walked in, holding letters they wanted Abbie's father to mail in town. The Indians slipped outside, but hung around the edges of the clearing.

"I can't go and leave my family with the Indians on the warpath," Rowland said. "We must tell the other settlers and prepare to defend ourselves."

Dr. Harriott shrugged and gazed out the window. The Indians prowled around outside. "I think they'll go home soon. Look, they're already gathering their things."

Rowland looked outside also, but he didn't seem to accept Dr. Harriott's opinion.

"Still, we should gather all the settlers here because this is the largest cabin and the strongest," Rowland said.

"Don't worry, they will go soon. Meanwhile, I have a few things I'd like to trade for before I go."

Abbie listened as the three men bartered and exchanged goods. Eventually, the neighbors returned to their own cabins. No one made any further mention of protecting the settlers against a possible attack.

The Sioux roamed about the area until noon. Then as Abbie watched, they drove off the family's small herd of cattle, shooting them as they went.

As soon as they were out of sight, Rowland turned to Harvey and a visiting settler named Mr. Clark. Abbie listened as they discussed whether they should try to warn the others. About 40 people lived in the Spirit Lake and Okoboji Lake area of Iowa at the time, including Abbie's family. Though it was a dangerous mission, Harvey and Mr. Clark determined they must try.

Mary wrapped her arms around her husband's neck and, with tears streaming down her face, cried, "O, Harvey! I am afraid you will never come back to me! The Indians will kill you if they don't any one else."

As the two men left, the clock chimed 2:00 p.m. An hour later the family heard shots coming from the house of the nearest neighbor, Mr. Mattock. Abbie prayed to God that her brother-in-law and his friend would return safely. The tension in the cabin grew with each passing hour. Finally, Abbie's father couldn't wait any longer.

"I'm going to find out what happened," he said. He stepped outside. Abbie and her mother, and the rest of the family, practically held their breath as they waited. Within a few moments he returned.

"Nine Indians are coming, now only a short distance from the house, and we are all doomed to die." He turned to bar the door and prepare to fight. "While they are killing all of us, I will kill a few of them, with the two loaded guns still left in the house."

"No, Rowland," Frances said quietly. She told them that she still hoped the Indians would spare them. "If we have to die, let us die innocent of shedding blood."

The door burst open and the Sioux swarmed inside, demanding flour. Rowland turned to give them the last of the family's supply. A warrior shot her father through the heart from the back. Abbie could only stare at the scene, unable to say or do anything. She saw him fall to the floor with a crash. Meanwhile, her sister Mary grabbed at the gun to tear it from the brave's hand. The other Indians grabbed both Mary and her mother and dragged them outside where Abbie could hear them being beaten to death.

Abbie, terrified, was rooted to her chair, clasping little Amanda against her, with little Rowland clinging to her skirts. She couldn't react: she couldn't speak or move. She only knew her parents and sister were dead, and the Indians were coming back.

The Indians began breaking everything in the house. They emptied the clothes from the trunks and cut open the feather beds, leaving the feathers to drift through the house.

An Indian approached Abbie and tore the two youngsters out of her clutching hands.

"Abbie, help us!" cried Rowland.

Abbie froze, she was so afraid. She heard the sound of the children being beaten outside. All her family was being killed around her and yet she remained. It wasn't fair for her to live.

She turned to the Indians still destroying the dishes and furniture. "Please, kill me!" she cried. The Indians ignored her, intent on their work. "Please, don't let me live without my family! Kill me, too!"

Finally, a brave grabbed her arm and dragged her to her feet. She could tell from his sign language that they were taking her with them. Their prisoner.

Her head filled with the awful stories she'd heard about how the Sioux treated their captives, and she knew her life would never be the same. If she survived.

She watched helplessly as they searched the house, keeping anything they felt they could use—bedding, guns, ammunition, food. Then they dragged her out of the house where her father's body still lay, past the beaten bodies of her mother and sister, and the still moaning and whimpering little ones, away into the night. She had no chance to even say good-bye to any of them. She only had one last look at their mangled bodies, surrounded by their own blood. At that moment the only thing she wanted in all the world was to die. But the Sioux had other plans. As night fell, they forced her to walk into the forest, following braves whose hands still dripped with blood, and with her mother's scalp dangling from one brave's belt.

When they reached Mr. Mattock's home, she saw campfires adding to the light of the burning cabin, lighting the night sky. Shrieks and groans pierced the clearing, and Abbie knew then there were still people inside. At least two, from the sound of their screams. Her eyes searched the area, seeing the bodies of Dr. Harriott and many others. All together the bodies of five men, two women, and four children sprawled about.

That night the Sioux celebrated their victory with a war-dance. They danced near the bodies lying on the blood-stained snow. They painted their faces black, then made wild screams and yells as they circled round and round until collapsing.

Abbie watched with terror in her heart. She was unable to sleep that night, afraid of every sound and movement.

The next morning the Sioux prepared for war, painting their faces black again, and went out to continue their slaughter. When the braves returned, they brought two more captives, Mrs. Noble and Mrs. Thatcher. The rest of the members of the four families they killed.

Abbie was taken to the tepee with the two women and left for a short time. They shared their stories and cried about what had happened and who had died. Then the Sioux took each of them to a separate lodge so they wouldn't have each other's company as comfort.

Once in the lodge, the squaws signaled for her to braid her hair and paint her face the way they did. Abbie had no desire to do so, but she knew she must or suffer. Once her hair was braided, the squaws rubbed oil into her hair and on her scalp. Now Abbie felt dirty and miserable as well as afraid.

She was in a tent one day, soon after her capture, when a warrior sitting beside her took his revolver from his belt and began loading it. He told her, using signs, that he meant to kill her as soon as it was loaded. Abbie wanted to die, to join her family, to not live in this fashion. She bowed her head to show that she was ready. The warrior pointed the gun at her head, and she again bowed her head, waiting for him to follow through with his threat. He lowered the gun, gazed at her for a moment in surprise, then broke out laughing. He kept laughing as others came into the tent, and he told them the story. After that, no one threatened her with a gun. She would remember that moment.

The snows were very deep that year, one of the worst winters ever. Abbie and the other captives were forced to carry heavy packs, weighing at least 70 pounds, without snowshoes. Abbie's pack contained eight bars of lead, one pint of lead balls, one tepee cover made of heavy cloth, one blanket, one bed comforter, one iron bar three feet long and one-half inch thick, one gun, and one piece of wood several inches wide and four feet long to keep the pack in shape. They were given moccasins to wear instead of their normal shoes so they wouldn't leave shoe prints in the snow.

The first day, Abbie drove a sleigh of horses, but only for one day. Then she was forced to walk.

The next day they broke camp and moved northwestwardly to Marble's Grove, on the west side of Spirit Lake. Here the Indians discovered another white family. Pretending friendship, the warriors gained entry and received a meal, then they killed Mr. Marble and captured his wife. They brought Mrs. Marble to the camp and gathered the captives together into one tepee. Then a group of warriors peeled the bark from a large tree and painted a picture story of the massacre on the white surface. That night they celebrated with another war-dance.

For the next week, Inkpaduta's band walked northwestward arriving at Heron Lake on March 26th. The warriors again painted their faces black, armed themselves each with a rifle and scalping knife, and left to attack Springfield, 15 miles away. Abbie feared for her sister, Eliza, who had gone to Springfield to work for another family during the fall of 1856.

Two days later the warriors returned bringing their captured goods: 12 horses, heavily laden with dry goods, groceries, powder, lead, quilts, clothing, and more. The warriors told Abbie they'd only killed one woman. She worried that it was her sister, but there was no way to know for certain.

The next morning the band started northwest again, heading for the unbroken wilderness. As the captives trudged along carrying their heavy packs through the deep snow, Abbie smiled to herself at how Mrs. Marble dealt with the papoose that had been added to her pack. The child was nearly two years old, wrapped in a blanket and seated in the top of the pack. When sleeping, the child was harder to carry. So, each time the Indians looked away, Mrs. Marble would claw the baby in the face to wake it up and make her load easier. Abbie was glad the child couldn't tell the Sioux what was wrong. After a while, Abbie helped Mrs. Marble keep watch for her chance to wake the baby.

The four women kept up as best they could, though they had never been raised to endure such hardship and torture. Mrs. Thatcher's health couldn't stand the strain of walking with the heavy packs through the cold and slushy snow. Abbie watched as her body deteriorated before her eyes, yet she was helpless to aid her.

A few days after the attack on Springfield, the Indians set up camp on a low piece of ground by a stream. Abbie saw everyone become excited and watchful. Abbie soon determined that soldiers had followed the band from Springfield. Maybe her release from this dreadful existence was near!

The braves kept a guard at the top of a hill. The squaws put out the fires and tore down the tepees. They packed up everything and, along with an injured brave and a sick papoose, scurried down the creek to hide in the shadows of the willows.

One brave hid at the base of a tree a short distance from camp, where he could see the movements of the pursuing soldiers as they neared the camp site. Abbie and the three other women were kept under guard, with orders to be killed if the soldiers attacked. Abbie's heart beat rapidly as they waited silently. She wanted to cry out to her salvation, but to do so meant certain death for herself and the others. She kept her mouth shut and waited. She realized she wanted to survive this horror for her family's sake.

More than an hour later, Abbie saw the soldiers turn and leave. She didn't know whether to be thankful or not. At least she was alive.

The braves quickly herded the captives down the creek to join the squaws and they deserted the camp. They walked for two days before setting up a camp in the afternoon. They had little food along the way. Such was the urgency of the band that the squaws were not given time to prepare anything to eat.

Midafternoon on the second day of the quick march, Abbie sank to the ground gratefully for a break with the rest of the band. But when they got up to move on, she couldn't rise. She was too weak and exhausted to go with them. The squaws urged her to follow, but she refused. Then one of the women ran back to her, waving a hoe of sorts over her head to get her to her feet. Abbie bowed her head, apparently prepared for the blow of the tool. The Sioux had spared her life before when she offered to die, maybe it would work again.

The squaw, now enraged that her threat didn't work, threw down her pack and grabbed Abbie's arm, jerking her to her feet. She adjusted Abbie's pack and roughly pushed her in the direction the rest of the band had already taken. Abbie stumbled along the path and soon arrived where the band had decided to set up camp for the night.

Each day proved to be the same torture as the band moved steadily northwest. When it came time to cross frozen rivers and streams, the Indians broke the ice with their horses. Then the squaws and captives waded through the waist-deep freezing water. Once on the other side, they kept walking with their wet clothes freezing to their bodies. At night, they laid down in the same clothes to sleep. Abbie was hungry all the time, as she was only given food every few days, and it was almost uneatable. She and the other captives were given food that the Indians didn't want. Abbie felt sorry for the poor horses that never had hay or grain to eat. Occasionally one would starve to death. Then the Indians would have meat for a few days. And the captives' packs grew heavier as the horse's load was divided among them.

Abbie tried to keep track of the passing days and weeks. She and the other captives marked each Sunday with prayers. After six weeks of the awful trek through the snow, across streams, rivers and lakes, the band arrived at the Big Sioux River. The river was swollen by the melting snows as spring finally arrived in Iowa.

As the band attempted to cross the river on a bridge of dead trees and debris, one Indian took Mrs. Thatcher's pack to carry for her. He urged her out onto the bridge. Abbie sensed something was wrong, for no one had offered to help any of the captives during the weeks of walking. Mrs. Thatcher turned to Abbie before stepping onto the bridge.

"Abbie, good-bye. This is my time. Please tell my dear husband and parents that I wanted to live and to escape for their sakes."

Abbie nodded, impressed by the 19-year-old woman's courage and endurance despite all her physical pains. She followed Mrs. Thatcher as they crossed to the center of the swollen stream. The young Sioux suddenly pushed Mrs. Thatcher from the bridge into the freezing water. She struggled for her life, and finally reached the shore they had just left, but other Indians threw clubs at her, and pushed her farther away from shore with long poles. Mrs. Thatcher tried to make it to the other shore, but as she approached she again was beaten back. Her strength failed and the strong current pulled her downstream. Abbie watched with tear-filled eyes as the Indians ran along the banks, yelling and throwing sticks and stones at the woman struggling in the water. As she finally came upon another pile of trees forming a bridge across the stream, she was shot and her body continued downstream.

Abbie knew then that death was likely near for her as well. The Sioux could kill her at any moment, with little or no reason. Abbie heard Mrs. Noble come up behind her and turned to face her. Mrs. Thatcher and Mrs. Noble were cousins, and Mrs. Noble was desperate to escape before meeting her cousin's fate.

"Abbie, we've got to end this. No one is going to save us! Let's go down the river and we can—we can drown ourselves, then they won't be able to torture us like this anymore."

"Mrs. Noble, how could we? They'd never let us get away."

"We can do it if we work together. Please! I don't want to die at their bloody, savage hands."

Abbie's heart ached with the deaths of her family and now Mrs. Thatcher. She had little hope of being rescued. Suddenly her mother's face came to mind, and she remembered what her mother had taught her about faith and hope. Her troubled soul calmed as she recalled her mother's voice and teachings. No matter what happened, she would survive.

"No, Mrs. Noble. I cannot," Abbie said. "We must have faith that we will be rescued."

On the sixth day of May, while camping about 30 miles west of the Big Sioux near Skunk Lake, or Chau-pta-ya-ton-ka as the Indians called it, Abbie saw two Sioux brothers come into camp. She learned later that they were Ma-kpe-ya-ha-ho-ton and Se-ha-ho-ta from the Yellow Medicine reservation in Minnesota. The next morning, the two men suggested buying Abbie. Abbie saw Inkpaduta shake his head, indicating she was not for sale. So they asked about buying Mrs. Marble. They made a deal and soon Mrs. Marble came to Abbie's tent to say good-bye.

"I think they're going to take me to white folk, Abbie," she said. "If so, I'll do all I can to get someone to come for you and Mrs. Noble." She hugged Abbie, then turned and left the tent.

Abbie watched as Mrs. Marble marched out of camp, four Indians in front while she marched behind in a single file line. She, like Abbie, wore the usual Indian costume: a calico chemise for a shirt, with an ankle-length skirt of blue broadcloth, gathered at the waist by a belt. Over the chemise and skirt, a length of blue and red broadcloth was worn as a wrap. Under the skirt, she wore blue pantalets and her moccasins.

After Mrs. Marble left, Abbie missed her. Now only Abbie and Mrs. Noble remained captive. Abbie grieved for Mrs. Thatcher, but she could only be thankful for Mrs. Marble's better situation.

The next day, Inkpaduta's band continued their journey farther beyond the Big Sioux, deep into Dakota territory. Abbie was forced to eat roots, like wild artichoke, to survive. Occasionally some wild game, such as geese, duck, swan, pelican or crane, were killed and eaten. At one point, the band went through an Indian village in Minnesota. Abbie was given a half teacup full of boiled corn—the first food she had eaten for three days.

One evening, just before sundown, a squaw came to Abbie and ordered her to go with her on a skunk hunt. The squaw carried a club, but Abbie went just to carry back the animal. Before long the squaw scented the skunk and just like a hound began to track it. She chased it into its hole and struck at it, but missed. Her club smashed into the ground, breaking it into pieces. She ordered Abbie to stay and guard the skunk to make sure it didn't escape, while she went to make a new club.

Abbie lay down by the hole to keep watch. She sighed as she settled down, glad to have a chance to rest. Watching the hole, she hoped the poor animal would escape. Within a short time, a small nose poked its way out of the hole. Abbie held still, afraid to breathe. The nose grew into a small face, the shiny eyes searching for signs of trouble. Apparently satisfied that he was safe, the skunk came out of the hole and left. Abbie let out her breath. Now she wouldn't have to eat him for supper. There were many foods she was forced to eat, but some she'd managed to hide and throw away, like the decaying fish they'd given her one evening.

The squaw returned just as dusk settled around them, and asked if the skunk was still in its hole.

Abbie shook her head and pointed in the direction that the little black and white animal had gone. The squaw began to yell at Abbie, gesturing with her hand and club how angry she was that Abbie had let their dinner escape. Abbie feared the club would land on her head or shoulders, but it didn't. Being too dark to continue the hunt, the squaw led the way back to camp.

Four weeks after Mrs. Marble left the camp, a small group of Yankton Indians joined Inkpaduta's band. After some debate, one of them, Wanduskaihanke, or End-of-the-snake, bought the captives. He was a one-legged man, and spent most of his time on his horse. Abbie learned that he wanted to sell her and Mrs. Noble to the whites to make money. Abbie hoped they would leave the band soon, on their journey back to her people. But End-of-the-snake wasn't in any hurry to part ways and traveled for some time with Inkpaduta.

Abbie and Mrs. Noble stayed in the same tepee. The small hope that her burdens would lessen died as Abbie found her situation exactly the same as before.

End-of-the-snake went on many hunting trips. Often Abbie was forced to go along to carry the game back to camp. If the game fell in the water, his dog would retrieve it and bring it to Abbie. Abbie didn't want to carry the dead animal, bloody and soaking wet, but she had no choice but lug it the miles back to camp.

A few evenings after Abbie was bought by End-of-the-snake, Abbie and Mrs. Noble prepared for bed. Suddenly Roaring Cloud came into the tent and ordered Mrs. Noble outside. She shook her head.

"You should go, he may kill you otherwise," Abbie urged.

"I don't care. I'm not going," Mrs. Noble said.

Roaring Cloud grabbed her arm with one hand, and a piece of firewood with the other, and dragged her outside. Abbie heard blows and groans from outside the tent. She listened in silence, knowing that if she tried to interfere she would receive the same treatment. Roaring Cloud came back into the tent and washed his bloody hands, then spoke to End-of-the-snake. Abbie's heart reached out to the woman dying just on the other side of the tepee skin, hearing her moans for a while, then silence. Abbie couldn't move, just like during her family's murder. Now she was alone with the Sioux. She had no one to share her sorrow or fear.

As the Indians went to sleep, and darkness surrounded the camp, Abbie buried her face in her hands and cried as she prayed. "Leave me not alone with these cruel savages! O God! Wilt thou leave me thus alone?" Abbie only wanted to be free of the terror and fear.

When dawn came, Abbie crawled from her makeshift bed. She heard a commotion outside, and suddenly remembered the acts of last night. She found herself dragged outside to watch as the Indians used Mrs. Noble's body for target practice. One warrior cut off Mrs. Noble's two braids and attached them to a stick. After the camp was packed, and the endless marching begun again, the warrior walked beside Abbie, lashing her with it in the face. She didn't know how she would survive, only that she must. She felt lonely and scared, and absolutely no one cared.

Suddenly that night, the tepee she was sleeping in was pulled down around her. She heard a great commotion outside, as she struggled to free herself from the bundle of skins. The camp was packed and ready to go in moments. The band left in a hurry and fled all night and all the next day. Abbie didn't know why they ran, or what they feared, she merely struggled to keep up.

Days passed. Each day carried them farther northwest. They crossed a vast prairie without trees of any kind. The band walked for miles and miles across an ocean of grasses, until Abbie began to wonder if she would ever see a tree again. The prairie was home to many animals, including fowl, birds, buffalo, and antelope.

Abbie upon her release, June 23, 1857. Sketch by Melody Gascho, based on a daguerreotype made that day.

One day the band passed a place where Abbie guessed a great battle had occurred. Several scaffolds reached eight or nine feet high, and stretched 15 feet long by six feet wide. The dead had been laid across the scaffolds, close together. Now only their bones remained, and those the wind had blown about. Abbie sat on the ground, exhausted and fearful, ignoring the discussion by the warriors about the dead. Finally, they started northwest again.

A few days later the band arrived at a large Indian village on the west bank of the James River. The river was beautiful, gracefully curving and looping, surrounded on both banks by trees, wild grape, and clinging vines. Abbie counted 190 lodges in the Yankton village. She guessed at least two thousand Indians lived there. Their clothes and tepees were made of buffalo robes. Abbie saw a woman walking toward her, naked. She looked away, and realized that many of the Sioux were naked. She had never been around people who were comfortable unclothed. She was glad when they led her into a tepee.

Upon seeing Abbie, the Yanktons gathered around the door of the tepee where she was staying. Some came in and looked at her, fingering her flaxen hair. She looked at them with her blue eyes, and they remarked at how they were different from their own brown ones. Abbie was uncomfortable with the attention. They made a big fuss over her lighter, though tanned, skin. A warrior from Inkpaduta's band rolled up her sleeve to show how white her skin was when she was first captured. Abbie saw that this fascinated them. She guessed she was the first white person they'd ever seen. The group's curiosity satisfied, they left, only to be followed by another group, then another.

Knowing that the band of Indians had continued to move farther and farther away from her home, Abbie finally gave up hoping to be rescued. Now she found herself in a place where there were no longer any signs of white man's clothing, weapons, or supplies. These Indians had never seen a white person. The small hope that Mrs. Marble might prompt Abbie's rescue also died. The death of Mrs. Noble had crushed the last ember of hope, to be replaced with despair. She was physically and emotionally exhausted. She had bruises and bumps, and now limped from the rough journey. Abbie had only the life of a slave before her. But at least she was alive.

After a couple days in camp, three Indians dressed in coats and starched white shirts came into Abbie's tent. These strange Indians, dressed as they were, caused a great deal of excitement in the village.

Abbie could tell immediately that they were from a white man's village. She found herself hoping again that she would be rescued. She didn't try to talk to them, though she wanted to. All she could do was watch, and wait. Before long she became aware that they were interested in her. Several councils were called, where the Indians talked. Abbie saw the Indians gather in her tepee, then go out to the prairie. They sat down in a circle, smoked, talked, smoked, and talked. Then they would walk about, talk, sit down in a circle, and talk. Abbie watched them do this for three days without knowing what was happening.

Inkpaduta's warriors tortured Abbie with tales of her being sold to the Indians so they could take her farther from her people and be killed. Abbie watched, horrified. Then realizing they were trying to upset her, she calmed her fears.

During the three days of discussion, one squaw finally told Abbie that the warriors' tales were not true. She was to be taken where white people lived. Abbie nodded, but she didn't know whom to believe. Her hopes and fears fought each other in her heart.

Finally the Indians agreed, and the visiting Indians paid the price to buy Abbie. She saw them hand over two horses, 12 blankets, two kegs of gun powder, 20 pounds of tobacco, 32 yards of blue squaw cloth, 37½ yards of calico and ribbon, and other small articles.

Abbie was given to her buyers, but they didn't leave immediately. First, they celebrated the deal with a dog feast—the highest honor in that tribe. Abbie could not bring herself to eat dog, so she stayed in her tent during the feast that lasted well into the night.

Early the next morning, the three Indians led Abbie out of the camp. She saw that two of the Yanktons, sons of End-of-the-snake, went with them to protect them from Inkpaduta's men. They put her into a buffalo-skin boat to cross the James River. Abbie briefly feared they meant to drown her, until they removed most of their clothes and guided the boat across the river. Was she on her way to civilization, or was it a trick to make her more willing to go with them?

Once on the other side of the river, Abbie was left with some of the Indians while others went and brought back a wagon and team of horses. They had hidden them so that the Yanktons and Inkpaduta didn't know they were there, and maybe want them for payment as well. Now they loaded the wagon with dried buffalo meat, buffalo robes, and other goods, while they asked Abbie to drive it. Then the five Indians, two from the Yankton village and three from the Yellow Medicine reservation, led Abbie in the wagon back east. She could not tell where they were going, but they were headed in the right direction. One Indian said "steamboat" to her, trying to tell her that they would be riding on a steamboat, but beyond that she couldn't tell.

The small group traveled for seven days before they reached an area where many Indians lived. Abbie saw log houses and her heart leapt with joy at the sight, thinking they were close to her people. When she reached the house, however, she found only Indians lived there and her heart fell. Was she to live among Indians forever?

Two days later they arrived at the house of a half-breed Indian who could speak English. Also living there were two girls who came to see Abbie. They invited Abbie to their house. When Abbie walked into the neat and tidy home, she saw the girls' father, a white man. Sitting on the floor was their mother, a full-blooded Sioux in full Sioux costume. She would not, by custom, eat with the family at the table.

During their meal, Abbie learned that the three Indians from Yellow Medicine were acting under agreement with the U.S. Indian agent, and that she was to be turned over to the Governor to be free.

Now at last, Abbie was safe and she could live her life in remembrance of her slain family. She vowed they would never be forgotten.

Just the Facts

Abigail Gardner was born in 1843 at Twin Lakes, Seneca County, New York. Her father was Rowland Gardner and her mother was Frances M. Smith Gardner. She had two sisters, Mary M. and Eliza M., and one younger brother Rowland. Her family moved to Iowa in 1855 to Clear Lake. Then in 1856 they moved farther west to Lake Okoboji and Spirit Lake. Additionally, the family included Mary's husband Harvey Luce, along with Mary and Harvey's two children, Albert (4 years) and Amanda (1 year).

The Spirit Lake Massacre occurred on March 8, 1857, at the end of a long, cold and snowy winter. Abigail was forced to watch her family be killed, then she was dragged off as a captive. She remained a captive for more than three months. The three women taken captive with her were Margaret Ann Marble, Lydia Noble, and Elizabeth Thatcher. Mrs. Marble was rescued May 21; Mrs. Noble and Mrs. Thatcher were murdered. Abbie was finally rescued by a band of Yankton Sioux who were representing the United States government.

Upon her release, she was turned over to Governor Sam Medary on Tuesday, June 23, 1857, at his room in the Fuller House, Shakopee, Minnesota. After several speeches, Major Flandreau presented to Abbie a war bonnet on behalf of Matowaken, the Yankton chief.

The war bonnet (or war-cap as she called it) is described by Abbie, in the *History of the Spirit Lake Massacre* (March 8, 1857), as:

> *a close fitting cap, of finely dressed buck-skin, soft and light. Around this was a crest of thirty-six of the very largest eagle-feathers, the quills being set with the utmost exactness, so as to form a true circle, wider at the top than at the base. Around the crest, the cap was covered with weasel fur, white as ermine, while the tails of weasels, equally as white, hung as pendants, all around, except in front. The tips of the feathers were painted black. Then there was a stripe of pink; then of black again; and the rest was pink.... To [the Sioux] every feather represented the high honor of having slain a fellow-mortal. The strangest thing about it was, that the great Yankton chieftain was willing to part with it. In so doing, he conferred the highest honor known to the Dakotas upon me.*

In all, 37 men, women, and children were killed during the massacre. Abbie was spared, she was told, because of her bravery.

Abbie was reunited with her sister Eliza on July 5. Eliza had married William Wilson and was living in Hampton, Franklin County, Iowa.

On August 16, 1857, Abbie married Casville Sharp. Eighteen months later she and her husband returned to Spirit Lake to the site of the massacre to visit the graves of her family. She found that someone else had taken over the claim and was living in the cabin her father had built. She was forced to leave without even being given her personal belongings. She and Casville returned to Hampton, then moved to Bremer County to land owned by Casville.

In 1859, their son Albert Sharp was born. They named him after Abbie's nephew, Albert, who had died at the massacre.

This photo originally appeared in History of the Spirit Lake Massacre and Captivity of Miss Abbie Gardner, written by Abbie Gardner Sharp in 1895.

They lived most of their lives in Iowa, though they spent some time living in Grundy County, Missouri. During the second stay, which lasted about a year, their house burned down, destroying everything they owned, including the Sioux war bonnet.

In 1860 they moved to Kansas and only lived there for a week before a drought forced them to move back to Iowa. There, in 1862, their son, Allen Sharp, was born.

Sometime later, they moved to Shell Rock, in Butler County, Iowa where in 1870 another fire destroyed everything in the house.

Their daughter, Minnie Sharp, was born in 1871. Eighteen months later the little girl died. Abbie said the loss of her child was the saddest event in her life since the massacre.

Abbie purchased the cabin at Spirit Lake in 1891, after the death of her husband. She removed a second story that had been added to it, and covered the exterior with lattice work. She ran a tourist attraction there, adding a gated entrance and charging admission. Abbie was instrumental in helping convince the government to erect a monument at the site in 1894 in memory of the victims and survivors of the massacre.

Abbie's health deteriorated over the years until she became an invalid confined to her room. She often spent months at a time unable to care for herself.

Abigail Gardner Sharp died from a paralyzing stroke on January 17, 1921 in Colfax, Iowa. She is buried with her family near her cabin.

Check It Out!

Gardner-Sharp, Abigail. *History of the Spirit Lake Massacre and Captivity of Miss Abbie Gardner*. New York: Garland Publishing Inc., 1976. Reprint from 1885 edition, Des Moines, Iowa Printing Co.

Lee, L.P. *History of the Spirit Lake Massacre! 8th March, 1857, and of Miss Abigail Gardiner's Three Month's Captivity Among the Indians.* New Britain: L.P. Lee, Publisher, 1857.

Teakle, Thomas. *The Spirit Lake Massacre.* Iowa City: State Historical Society of Iowa, 1918.

Contact the State Historical Society of Iowa (402 Iowa Avenue, Iowa City, IA 52240-1806) for a collection of articles about Abbie.

Wait 'Til You See This!

The Abbie Gardner Cabin Historic Site is located on Monument Drive, one block west of Arnolds Park Amusement Park in Arnolds Park, Iowa. Also at this site is a 55-foot granite obelisk monument to those involved in the massacre. A museum is located near the cabin and is open every day from Saturday, Memorial Day weekend through October 1st. Hours are 9 a.m.–4 p.m weekends, and 12 p.m.–4 p.m. weekdays. For more information, contact the local manager at Box 74, Arnolds Park, Iowa 51331. Or call 712-332-7248.

Other Sources

Arnold, Vinton. "Tells of his friendship with Abbie Gardner Sharp." *Messenger.* Fort Dodge. May 9, 1971.

"Abbie Gardner Sharp Dead." *Rutheun Free Press.* January 26, 1921.

"Abbie Gardner Sharpe, Survivor Spirit Lake Massacre, Is Dead." *Des Moines Capital.* January 24, 1921.

"Death of Arnolds Park Woman Calls Up Historic Event." *Mason City Gazette.* January 29, 1921.

"Death of Survivor of Indiana Massacre." *Woodbine Twiner.* February 10, 1921.

Editorial Department. *Annals of Iowa*. "Notable Deaths." 229-30. [full citation unavailable; provided by State Historical Society of Iowa.]

History of Emmet County and Dickinson County, Iowa. Volume I. Chicago: The Pioneer Publishing Company, 1917.

"Iowa D.A.R. Opposed to Sharpe Memorial." *Des Moines Tribune*. March 23, 1921.

"Last Survivor Dead." *Forrest City Summit*. January 27, 1921.

"Massacre Survivor is No More." *Estherville Republican*. January 26, 1921.

Petersen, William J. "Westward with the Gardners." *The Palimpsest*. Vol XLIII. No. 10. State Historical Society of Iowa, October 1962.

Sherr, Lynn and Jurate Kazickas. *Susan B. Anthony Slept Here: A Guide to American Women's Landmarks*. 145-146. New York: Random House, 1994.

"...Should Be Preserved." *Boone News-Republican*. Friday, September 7, 1951. [Article about preserving the Abbie Gardiner cabin.]

"Sole Survivor of Spirit Lake Indian Massacre Passes." *Marshalltown Times-Republican*. January 24, 1921.

"Survivor of Spirit Lake Massacre Ill." *Perry Tribune*. October 23, 1919.

United Press International. "Log cabin piques interest of owners." August 23, 1987. United Press International. Distributed in Iowa, regional section.

[Untitled: Dateline Des Moines, IA, Jan 25.] *Council Bluffs Nonpareil*. January 25, 1921.

JANE SILCOTT

1860

Leading the Way

Jane looked at the elders and white men seated inside the large lodge. Their eyes were serious and fixed on her father, Chief Timothy, who was trying to convince the white men to go back to their own territory. She watched her mother, Fannie, while listening quietly to the awkward discussion. One white man, Captain Pierce, didn't speak the Nez Perce language, so the chief made motions with his hands to talk. They'd been "talking" for hours and still Pierce would not leave.

"Better go back," Chief Timothy said, pointing in the direction of the sunset. Jane watched as her father told Pierce he would likely be shot through the heart and his scalp taken by Indians defending their homeland.

Jane listened without comment. She knew that the white men were breaking their own law by crossing onto the Indian lands. She also heard Pierce say they were looking for the gold everyone guessed was up the Clearwater River.

Pierce frowned. He suggested they go up the trail at night.

Chief Timothy shook his head.

Pierce asked if there were another trail they could follow.

The old chief traced a line on his open hand, showing that it would take two days toward the snow, then several days toward the rising sun.

Then he showed the trail dying out and the white men getting lost. Jane leaned forward as she recognized the path her father described.

Once lost, the old chief went on, they would have to follow the river downstream, right into the path of the angry Indians. The chief showed them being killed at that point as well. No, no good way for them to go up the river to find what they were looking for. Only an Indian could find the trail.

Pierce nodded. "Is there any chance of finding a guide who could show us the trail?"

"No," Chief Timothy said. "I am the white man's friend. But I've never been paid for the horses and canoes that I gave to another man for his fight. I lost my son Big Lion because of my friendship with the white man. Now all my men are being watched. If one of us went with you, we would certainly die. If we cannot go, who could?"

Silence met his question with only the crackle of the fire to interrupt.

"I will go," Jane said calmly. She braced herself for the Council's reaction.

Shocked silence echoed around the council as the men realized a woman had dared speak.

"Jane, no. I will not lose you too," Chief Timothy said. He looked at her with a mix of shock and pride.

"I can do it, father," Jane replied.

A great commotion grew within the lodge as the council members discussed the idea. They tried to talk her out of taking such a dangerous trip. She would not change her mind. The white men had always been her friends as well. They had given her the name Jane when she was just one year old. They had taught her at the Spalding Mission school, and she learned about their God. She felt that white men brought good to her people, and she wanted to help them now. She would show them the way.

As the commotion settled, Jane noticed Pierce smiling, as were his five companions.

"Does the girl know the trail?" asked Pierce.

Jane Silcott. Courtesy Idaho State Historical Society, 80.54.11.

Jane's black eyes crinkled into a smile, relieving her usual stern expression. "She knows every mountain and creek, every meadow and good camping spot," Chief Timothy said.

Jane had hiked all over the mountains during the hunt for camas and couse roots. She had helped keep the camp while the braves hunted, and she had dressed the skins and smoked the meat they brought back. Of course she knew the trail!

The next evening, as the sun was setting, Pierce and his party met Jane at the river. Her black hair, hanging below her shoulders, moved in the gentle breeze. Chief Timothy's canoes waited for them to cross the river in the dark. They wrapped the paddles to muffle them in the water.

Once across, Jane led them up a dry ravine to the plateau of land above. She led them alongside the old Lapwai trail, keeping some distance away from it as they walked.

When the sun began to rise, they rested in a small hollow, hiding in the brush until dusk. Then they started walking again, coming to what today is called Moscow, Idaho. They turned and went around the Thatuna Hills and waded across the Potlatch river.

"Now it is safe to travel by day," Jane said to the men. She led them down the hill, walking through the white pine forests that stretched for miles. They crossed the North Fork at the mouth of Swamp Creek without any trouble. Jane walked confidently. The white men stumbled over rocks and branches as they attempted to follow her. She led them along Reed's Creek down to a little stream known as Canal Gulch. Picking their way along the stream edge, stepping over branches and stones, they walked to the mouth of the stream to where it met Orofino Creek.

"We'll camp here," Jane said. She began to set up camp.

One man went to catch fish for dinner. Another started a cooking fire. When the meal was finished, Jane cleaned the dishes while the exhausted men sat by the fire and smoked, gazing at the beautiful scenery before them. The Orofino murmured down a long hill starting above their camp, cutting between two green meadows, before plunging into a series of rapids and cascades. The tall pine trees stood sentry in the distance. Jane busied herself around the camp as the sun slowly set.

Jane saw one of the men, W. F. Basset, quietly stand up, take his pan and shovel, and walk back up Canal Gulch until he was out of sight of the group. She wondered what he would do when it was dark, but didn't say anything to the rest of the men who continued talking by the fire.

A yell pierced the peaceful setting. The group of men glanced at each other and jumped to their feet. Soon they were running up Canal Gulch after Bassett. Jane followed them. What had he found? When she came around the bend in the river, she saw Bassett standing with his pan tilted before him, looking down at its contents. His face had lost its color, shocked at what he saw. When Jane got closer, she saw small gold grains within the pan of water, and her face broke into a smile. He had found the gold and now more white men would come.

Just the Facts

Jane Silcott was born into the lower branch of the Nez Perce tribe in 1842. It is believed she was born in Idaho, where the Clearwater river (Koos-koos-kie) meets the Snake river (Ki-moo-ee-nem), in a valley just below their junction.

Her father was subchief Ta-moot-sin, who later became Timothy when he converted to Christianity. He died in 1890 in poverty.

Her mother converted to Christianity in 1843. She came to the Spalding Mission, where she was called Fannie, and her one-year-old little girl, Jane.

Jane had a sister who later married a Yakima Indian named George Waters, and a brother called Big Lion, who was later named Edward by the whites.

Jane grew up in a valley below present-day Lewiston, Idaho, where Alpowa Creek (a small stream) meets the Snake River. Silcott post office used to be located there. Timothy Memorial Bridge, named after Jane's father, was built across Alpowa Creek.

Jane had black hair, black eyes, high cheekbones, and was normally quiet and seldom expressed emotion.

In August 1860, a group of white men came to Jane's father for help. The group was led by E. D. Pierce, an adventurer who had lived among the Indians for many years as a trapper and trader. W. F. Bassett who found the first grains of gold, Thomas Walters, Jonathon Smith, and John and James Dodge were the other prospectors. They were trespassing according to federal law, but their desire for gold spurred them on. Only after the group discussed options with the chief for most of the evening, did Jane volunteer to guide them. She led them to the rivers where the stories of gold started.

The place where the gold was found became a town known today as Pierce, Idaho. Thus the state of Idaho was born.

After Bassett discovered the gold grains, the group stayed a day or so and collected 80 dollars in gold dust before going back to Walla Walla, with Jane leading them.

It is believed that when Jane and the group reached Lapwai, she noticed John Silcott for the first time. He was supervising the progress of construction on the Indian Agency where he worked. As time went on, Jane and her people spent a lot of time in Lapwai where the government began carrying out the terms of the treaties. John Silcott made sure the building of shops and schools was on schedule.

Jane married a half-blood Nez Perce, though his name is not recorded in any sources. She had one boy by this marriage, but the boy drowned.

After her first husband died (of what, no one says), Jane married John Silcott. John originally came from Virginia. In 1860 he was 36 years old. The couple ran a ferry boat across the Clearwater at Lewiston for many years.

Jane died on the evening of January 17, 1895 after drinking too much alcohol, and when she tried to do something at the fireplace—perhaps add a log or stir the embers—she either fell into it or her long skirts caught on fire, and she burned to death. She was 53 years old. She and John are buried side by side on a hill overlooking the Clearwater and Snake rivers.

A marble monument was erected at the site by John before he died in 1902 at Walla Walla, Idaho.

Check It Out!

Defenbach, Byron. *Idaho: The Place and Its People.* Chicago: The American Historical Society, Inc., 1933.

Defenbach, Byron. *Red Heroines of the Northwest.* Caldwell: Caxton Printers, Ltd., 1929. Third Printing March 1935.

Defenbach, Byron. *The State We Live In: Idaho.* Caldwell: Caxton Printers, Ltd., 1933.

Online Resources

For information about the Nez Perce National Historical Park, go to *www.nps.gov/nepe/.*

Wait 'Til You See This!

A marble monument to Jane and her husband John Silcott was built at their gravesites outside of Lewiston. It is north of the Clearwater River, near where it joins the Snake River. A marker is there, but her casket has been removed due to vandalism.

Other Sources

Luchetti, Cathy. *Women of the West.* St. George: Antelope Island Press, 1982. [Includes a photo of Jane Silcott]

Penson-Ward, Betty. *Who's Who of Idaho Women of the Past.* 32. Boise: Idaho Commission on Women's Programs, 1981.

Sherr, Lynn and Jurate Kazickas. *Susan B. Anthony Slept Here: A Guide to American Women's Landmarks.* 125-126. New York: Random House, 1994.

Spangenburg, Ray and Diane K. Moser. *The American Indian Experience.* New York: Facts On File, Inc., 1997.

GRACE BEDELL BILLINGS

1860

The Girl Who Changed the Face of Lincoln

A huge black train chugged into the Westfield, New York station on a cold February day in 1861. Decorated with banners and red, white and blue streamers, the train proclaimed that a presidential candidate was on board. As it drew to a halt, young Grace waited nervously, clutching a bouquet of roses to give to the important man she admired so much, Abraham Lincoln. Soon, sporting a new beard, he stepped onto the rear platform and waited for the clapping and cheering to stop.

Grace held her breath. The moment had finally come when she would meet this man, the man she had dared to suggest grow a beard. She remembered impulsively sitting down to write the short note to him last October. She could recite it word for word even now.

Westfield, Chatauqua Co., N.Y.,
Oct. 15, 1860

Hon. A. Lincoln
Dear Sir:
    My father has just come from the fair and brought home your picture and Mr. Hamlin's. I am a little girl only eleven years old, but want you should be President of the United States very much so I

hope you won't think me very bold to write to such a great man as you are. Have you any little girls about as large as I am if so give them my love and tell her to write to me if you cannot answer this letter. I have got 4 brothers and part of them will vote for you any way and if you will let your whiskers grow I will try and get the rest of them to vote for you you would look a great deal better for your face is so thin. All the ladies like whiskers and they would tease their husbands to vote for you and then you would be President. My father is a going to vote for you and if I was a man I would vote for you to but I will try and get every one to vote for you that I can.... When you direct your letter direct to Grace Bedell Westfield Chatauqua County New York. I must not write any more answer this letter right off Good bye.

Grace Bedell

She had been thrilled to receive his letter shortly afterward. She couldn't even wait to get home to open it. As she hurried home in the snow from the post office she tore open the envelope and saw that Lincoln's letter was dated just four days after her own. He had really written back right away! The snow flakes falling furiously from the sky had landed lightly on the page as she read his words.

Private
Springfield, Ill., Oct. 19, 1860

Miss Grace Bedell
My dear little Miss:

Your very agreeable letter of the 15th is received.

I regret the necessity of saying I have no daughter. I have three sons—one seventeen, one nine, and one seven years of age. They with their mother, constitute my whole family.

As to the whiskers, having never worn any, do you not think people would call it a piece of silly affect[at]ion if I were to begin it now?

Your very sincere well-wisher,
A. Lincoln

And now here the tall, thin man stood waiting for silence in her own hometown.

"I have a young correspondent in this town," Abraham Lincoln said. "Please bring her to the platform if she is here."

This memorial park shows Grace holding her bouquet of flowers as she greets Abraham Lincoln. Photo by Chris Bolté.

The people of the town of Westfield, New York, glanced around and spotted Grace waiting to be introduced. She walked on trembling legs to the platform, her palms wet against the stems of the flowers. She was ushered quickly through the crowd and helped onto the metal platform to stand beside Lincoln. She could not get her breath, she was so nervous.

Lincoln looked down at her with a kind smile, a glint of laughter in his eyes. He reached down and swooped her into the air.

"See Gracie, I've raised some whiskers just for you!"

The watching crowd of Grace's neighbors and friends roared their approval, clapping as loudly as they could. She couldn't wait to get home and tell her mother all about what had just happened. Once more on her feet, Grace excitedly dashed off the platform, scooted under a wagon, out the other side, and raced home. It was only as she approached her own front door that she realized she still carried the gift of flowers, now without any pink or red petals, in her hand.

Just the Facts

Grace was born in Albion, New York, on November 4, 1848.

Her father was Norman Bedell, a stove maker, who was born in Genesee County, New York, in 1809. He had ancestors who fought in the American Revolution.

Her mother was Amanda Smiley. She was born in Batavia, New York, in 1813. She died at Bowmansville, New York, in 1879.

Grace [RTF annotation: Who were her brothers and sisters?]had nine brothers and sisters. Her family moved to Westfield for only a few years, but long enough for Grace to "change the face of Lincoln." Then they moved back to Albion and she attended the Albion Academy until 1863, then attended Phipps Union Seminary in 1864. She graduated from the Albion Academy in 1866.

Albion is where she met her husband, George Newton Billings, a veteran of the Civil War. George was born at East Gaines, New York, December 7, 1845. He had served with the 8th New York Heavy Artillery and the 10th New York Infantry as a sergeant from 1863 until 1866. Newton and Grace were married on December 3, 1867, in Albion. They moved to Delphos, Kansas, in 1870, where they became one of the first settling families. Life wasn't easy on the prairie. They fought swarms of grasshoppers, tornadoes, grass fires that swept the prairie, drought, blizzards, fevers, and money problems. Of course, life wasn't all bad out there, for they loved the wide open spaces, the sunsets, and the people they met.

Grace and George had one son, Harlow Billings, who was born on September 16, 1872 in Delphos. He grew up and married Ellarene Bishop.

Grace lived in Delphos, Kansas, for the rest of her life, and kept a close eye on political and foreign affairs, as well as football and baseball. She was known as the "grandma of everybody in town."

She didn't become known to the world until Robert Todd Lincoln's widow found her letter among Robert's papers. Before long, the press was fascinated by the story. The letters were published in a collection of Abraham Lincoln's letters, *Dear Mr. Lincoln: Letters to the President.*

George died on June 23, 1930 in Delphos. Grace died at the age of 88 on November 2, 1936, in Delphos, Kansas.

Even though Grace never saw Lincoln again, their letter writing lives on to this day. Historians suggest that the beard helped Lincoln appear as more of a father figure to the soldiers who were called on to fight the Civil War, making it easier for them to want to fight for him. Others think the beard made Lincoln look worse. Either way, Grace's short note to a presidential candidate changed the way Lincoln faced our nation, and forever changed the appearance of our 16th president.

The Chautauqua County Executive Andrew Goodell, Mayor Joseph Pagano, and Westfield Supervisor David Ross declared Tuesday, November 9, 1993 "Lincoln-Bedell Day" in Westfield, New York.

The original letter was sold by Grace's descendants to a New York TV producer, David Wolper, on March 22, 1966 for $20,000.

Check It Out!

Fiction

Pauli, Hertha Ernestine. *Lincoln's Little Correspondent.* Garden City, New York: Doubleday, 1952.

Roop, Connie. *Grace's Letter to Lincoln.* New York: Hyperion Books, 1998.

Trump, Fred. *Lincoln's Little Girl: A True Story.* Honesdale: Boyds Mill Press, 1994.

Winnick, Karen B. *Mr. Lincoln's Whiskers.* Honesdale: Boyds Mills Press, 1996.

Nonfiction

Dondero, George Anthony. *Why Lincoln Wore a Beard.* Springfield: pub unknown, 1931.

Greenberg, Judith E. *Young People's Letters to the President.* Danbury: Grolier Publishing, 1998.

Wait 'Til You See This!

A granite monument bearing copper reproductions of both letters stands in the Delphos, Kansas, town square.

THE LINCOLN-BEDELL STATUE PARK
ESTABLISHED JULY 10, 1999

THE MEETING OF PRESIDENT-ELECT ABRAHAM LINCOLN AND HIS
FAMOUS CORRESPONDENT, TWELVE-YEAR-OLD GRACE BEDELL TOOK
PLACE ON FEBRUARY 16, 1861, IN WESTFIELD AT THE TRAIN
STATION. PRIOR TO THIS, GRACE HAD PENNED A LETTER TO
LINCOLN SUGGESTING THAT WHISKERS WOULD IMPROVE HIS APPEARANCE.
AT THEIR MEETING, LINCOLN SHOOK HER HAND, KISSED GRACE, AND
ASKED HER HOW SHE LIKED THE IMPROVEMENTS SHE HAD ADVISED.

THE STATUES ARE THE WORK OF SCULPTOR DON SOTTILE, A NATIVE
OF WESTFIELD. THE BRONZE CASTING TOOK PLACE AT THE FIREWORKS
FOUNDRY, PENN YANN, UPSTATE NEW YORK.

WESTFIELD IS MOST GRATEFUL TO TOWN HISTORIAN BILLIE
DIBBLE FOR THE INSPIRATION AND DR. KENT L. BROWN FOR
GUIDING THE PROJECT THROUGH TO COMPLETION.

This marker in Westfield, New York, tells the story of Grace's correspondence with the president. Photo by Chris Bolté.

A monument, showing Grace with her bouquet and Abraham Lincoln facing each other, was dedicated in July 1999 at the four main corners in Grace's hometown of Westfield, New York, along Main Street.

Other Sources

Balch, William Monroe. "She Changed the Face of Lincoln." *Wichita Eagle*. May 2, 1937. [From Abraham Lincoln, Clippings. V.1., Kansas Historical Society.]

Baldwin, Sara Mullin and Robert Morton Baldwin, editors. *Illustriana Kansas: Biographical Sketches of Kansas Men and Women of*

Achievement Who Have Been Awarded Life Membership in Kansas Illustriana Society. 106-7. Hebron: Illustriana Inc., 1933.

Buyer, Bob. "Efforts of Four Volunteers Prompt Growth Movement in Westfield." *The Buffalo News*. May 30, 1995. Local Section, 5C.

Harper, Robert S. *Lincoln and the Press*. 85. New York: McGraw-Hill Book Co., Inc., 1951.

Hillinger, Charles. "Preserving Memory of 3 Noted Kansas Women." *The Los Angeles Times*. October 19, 1986, Home Edition, View Section. 10, column 1.

Holzer, Harold, Gabor S. Boritt, Mark E. Neely, Jr. *The Lincoln Image: Abraham Lincoln and the Popular Print*. 71-3. New York: Scribner Press, 1984.

"Lincoln's Little Girl Back in the News with Complete Story Told in New Children's Book." *PR Newswire*. Thursday, February 10, 1994.

Salmagundi. Editorial. *The Baltimore Sun*. August 17, 1994. Wednesday, Final Edition, 18A.

Sherr, Lynn and Jurate Kazickas. *Susan B. Anthony Slept Here: A Guide to American Women's Landmarks*. 155-6. New York: Random House, 1994.

Shumaker, Anna Mae. "She Changed Lincoln's Face." *Baldwin Ledger*. April 23, 1936. [From Abraham Lincoln, Clippings. V.1., Kansas Historical Society.]

"Lincoln-Bedell Day Set in Chautauqua County." *The Buffalo News*. Friday, November 5, 1993, Local Section.

Tullai, Martin D. "Lincoln Still Towers Above Other Presidents." *The Washington Times*. Saturday, February 13, 1993. Part B, B3.

MARY KATE PATTERSON

1861

Mother's Last Good Dish

Wrapping the reins around the brake, Kate stepped down from the carriage in front of her parents' home in Rashboro, Tennessee. The nine-mile drive didn't normally take so long, but the Yankees had set up posts between Nashville and Rashboro. The guards had questioned her at length as to why she was traveling alone and where she was going. They'd searched her carriage from one end to the other, leaving only her own person untouched.

She had mixed feelings about being home. She was sad because she'd left the excitement of attending the Elliott School in Nashville, leaving many new friends behind. She could only hope that the Civil War would end soon. Maybe she'd get to see her friends sometimes. She sighed as she gazed at the cozy farmhouse before her. As always, it felt good to come home.

Suddenly her cousin, Robbie, ran from the house. Her pretty face and slim figure had grown up a bit more while Kate was at school. Yet she was still acting like a girl, running across the lawn. Her mother would not like to see that, but it made Kate smile even bigger.

"Kate! I'm so glad you're back!" Robbie cried, racing to the gate.

"Robbie, it's good to see you, too," Kate replied, hugging her friend.

"Come, your mother is waiting for you inside," Robbie said.

Kate strode arm and arm with Robbie across the lawn and into the house, her chocolate-colored curls bouncing with each step.

"She's home!" Robbie called as they entered the coolness of the house. The smell of fresh bread came from the kitchen, making both girls hurry in that direction.

They walked into the log kitchen to find Kate's mother pulling golden loaves of bread from the brick oven. Ellen Patterson smiled at them as she set the pans on top of the stove, then hurried to Kate.

"How was your trip? Any problems?" Her mother gave her a quick hug, and held her by the shoulders for a moment, assessing her appearance.

"No, it was fine. It's good to be home." Kate let her eyes roam the kitchen, up to the loft. How many times had she and Robbie laid up there and listened to the conversations at the dining room table? My, it was good to be home!

As the days went by, Kate wasn't sure how she was supposed to spend her time. She didn't have any studies to do because the war had closed the school. Her parents wanted her at home. She wanted to do something to help the South win their fight. But what?

One day, her father suggested they take a walk. Dr. Hugh Patterson enjoyed his daily strolls, and Kate enjoyed walking with him. But there was something on his mind this time. Kate paced silently beside him, waiting.

"Kate," he said finally, "I'm sorry you had to leave school. Your education is so important. We'll have to make arrangements for you to finish your schooling here. But for now, I need to ask your help."

A chill wiggled down Kate's spine. She straightened her back and lifted her chin. Her deep brown eyes peered at him.

"Anything, father."

"You know that our boys need medicine, and that the roads are guarded by Yankees. I need your help getting the morphine and quinine to them, to lessen their pain."

Kate's house in LaVergne, Tennessee. Photo by Betty Bolté.

Kate thought for only a moment before answering. All of her family, and that of her uncle's nearby, were already involved in aiding the Rebels. She remembered the Yankees searching her buggy, and not searching her. "I can hide the medicine in my riding habit. When do I need to leave?"

Dr. Patterson smiled grimly, fully aware of the danger in which he was placing his daughter. If she was caught smuggling the medicine across the Union lines, it would mean her death.

"Tomorrow morning I'll have the extra medicines I need and the pass for you to go to Nashville. You can leave after breakfast." He started to walk away, but Kate's hand on his arm stopped him.

"Father, thank you for trusting me to get the medicine through. I can do that much for our boys."

The next morning she set out with the packets of drugs hidden around her waist. Her heart beat fast as she stepped into her buggy. The wounded soldiers needed the medicine she carried. She slapped the reins on the horse's back and started for the Union lines.

She drove at an easy pace, making sure it looked like she was simply out for a drive. She was in no apparent hurry, while inside she wanted to gallop the horse through the lines.

When she reached the sentry, a soldier examined her pass. Kate forced herself to breathe normally as he read the piece of paper. Then the soldier searched the buggy. Finding nothing, he waved her through. She let out her breath and smiled too herself. That wasn't so bad.

Over the next several months, Kate made many trips to Nashville. Often her cousin Robbie went with her. Kate made sure she knew who the commanding officer was, and became friendly with him. Then she would ask for a pass to visit a friend at the Elliott School in Nashville. The officer readily granted the request.

Little did the commander know that Kate had her buggy fitted with a false bottom where she could hide large supplies for the Rebel soldiers. She'd smuggle cavalry boots, bridles, spurs, blankets, and more through the Union lines.

Working together the girls sweet-talked information from Yankee soldiers. The men, so far from home and their own girlfriends, enjoyed chatting with the girls. Before long, they'd let slip some tidbit of information on where the Union army was heading, or how many soldiers were in a certain platoon.

As the war progressed, her father became even more involved in the spy network for the South. The house on Nolensville Road, in Rashboro, became an important underground headquarters for the Confederate scouts. Between Dr. Patterson's connections in Rashboro and LaVergne, and Kate's friends in Nashville, they were able to keep the Southern soldiers informed of the Yankees' whereabouts.

During their trips, Kate and Robbie became aware of a young man who claimed to be a cattle buyer. They kept a wary eye on him. Before long they realized he never had any cows with him. They reported him to the Confederate scouts, who tried to find out if the man was a Yankee spy.

Mary Kate Patterson. Courtesy Marian Herndon Dunn.

Kate saw the cattle buyer across the street one afternoon when she and Robbie were in Nashville. She tracked his progress, until he suddenly turned toward them.

"He's coming this way," Kate said.

"I see him," Robbie replied, pulling her shawl more tightly about her. "Should we speak to him?"

"Yes, see what we can find out about the Yankee troops moving out this morning," Kate said quickly as the man stopped in front of them.

"Good day, Miss Patterson, Miss Woodruff," he said, tipping his hat in salute.

"Good day, sir," the girls replied.

"What brings you into town on such a cold December day?"

"A little Christmas shopping," Kate replied. Luckily, she had a small bag of goodies she'd picked up to take home. Nothing fancy, just some small candies.

The "cattle buyer" talked to them, and asked them several questions about how the Rebels were faring. Kate bit back her disgust at his attempt to get information from them. The girls answered his questions with apparent openness and honesty. Actually, they told him lies about the Rebels' position and welfare, lies he would most likely take back to the Yankee camp.

"I understand your mother might have a cow she'd like to sell," he said, finally. "Maybe I'll stop by and talk to her about it."

"I'm sure she'd talk to you about it, but don't get your hopes up," Kate said. She hoped he didn't come to the house, if he was really a spy like she thought. She never knew when the scouts would stop by, and she wouldn't want the spy and the scouts to meet.

A few weeks went by while Kate's friends tried to determine if the cattle buyer was indeed a spy, or just a bad cattle buyer. They couldn't.

Then on Christmas Eve, 1862, Kate placed a lamp in the agreed window, signaling that the house was safe to approach. Two Confederate soldiers walked up quietly, leaving a third man a safe distance away hiding their horses. Private Richard Adams came in through the back door, leaving Private Jake McCain as guard outside.

"Private Adams," Kate said as he came in, "I'm glad you made it safely. That rascal has been here twice. Once last night, and again this morning, trying to talk mother into selling her cow. But she won't."

Before Adams could reply, the soldier outside called to him.

"Adams!" McCain called from outside the door, "someone is approaching from behind the house."

"Come in here, then, McCain," Private Adams said.

Kate peeked out the window through the curtains. "It's that cattle buyer again," she said. "He's surely coming back here."

Adams glanced around and spied the loft above the log kitchen. "Up there," he said. Adams and McCain soon were out of sight. Kate shook her head at the irony; how many times had she herself hidden up there?

A loud knock at the door rang through the house. Mrs. Patterson answered it, knowing already who it was.

"Good afternoon, Mrs. Patterson," the man said. "I am so very hungry. Might you have some dinner I could enjoy?"

"Of course," Mrs. Patterson said, looking meaningfully at the girls. "I'd be happy to fix you something. Just come inside, out of the cold. Girls, please?"

Kate and Robbie played hostess to the spy, chatting with him about the weather, and the holidays, and whatever came to mind. Mrs. Patterson busied herself in the kitchen.

The girls flattered the cattle trader enough that he began to brag to the young misses about watching the Confederates and reporting their movements to the Yankees. Adams and McCain listened carefully to all he said.

"Have you seen any suspicious characters around here?" he asked.

"I saw Private Richard Adams and three other Confederates just this morning," Mrs. Patterson said, coming into the room. "They seemed to know a good bit about what was going on in the Southern army. I believe they were headed toward LaVergne, coming from Nashville."

Kate saw Adams signal that they would come down and capture the spy. She nodded, pretending to agree with what the trader was saying.

"Come have your dinner, sir," Mrs. Patterson said.

While he ate, they kept up the conversation. Adams and McCain descended from the loft. Adams made it down quietly, but McCain managed to make a bit of noise.

One of the girls "accidentally" dropped a large plate on the floor, covering the sound.

"My best platter!" Mrs. Patterson cried loudly. She jumped up from the table, upsetting her chair so that it crashed to the floor.

During this commotion, the Yankee spy continued to eat like a man starved for weeks. As he stabbed another bite of meat, he felt the cold steel of two muzzles on his head.

"Take off your gun belt, and leave your arms at your side," one of the Rebel soldiers ordered.

"I'm just a farmer trying to finish a fine meal," the trader replied.

"You can't treat a guest in my house so rudely," Mrs. Patterson said, trying not to smile.

"Do as I say Yank, or you'll regret your stubbornness," the Rebel soldier commanded.

"How can you arrest him while he's eating, for heavens sakes!" cried Kate, on her feet.

Robbie stood to one side, pretending to be afraid of the soldiers.

The Yankee spy threw his gun belt, containing two Colt army pistols, to the floor. McCain searched the man, finally pulling out a set of papers. At first, McCain thought they were merely papers with cattle trading notes on them. Looking more closely, however, he realized what he was reading was a code for the Southern army movements and position. Adams and McCain soon had the Yankee spy out of the house on his way to the Southern army's headquarters.

After the soldiers left, the three women looked at each other and smiled.

"Good work, ladies," Mrs. Patterson said to the girls.

"You should have been on the stage," Robbie said to Kate. "How dare you barge in here…!"

Kate laughed, knowing she'd helped once again in her own small way, to fight the war for the South.

Just the Facts

Mary Kate Patterson, known as Kate, was born on October 15, 1844, in Warren County, Kentucky. (Some sources say she was born in 1838.) Her parents were Dr. Hugh and Ellen T. Patterson. In 1850 her family moved to Rashboro, in Rutherford County, Tennessee. Rashboro was located near LaVergne, Tennessee.

Kate had five brothers: Everand Meade Patterson, a member of the Coleman's Scouts during the Civil War, Robert, James, Hugh, and Charlie, who became a doctor. She also had one sister, Margaret.

The Patterson farm became one of the most important gathering places for the Confederate scouts. They had a system of signals they used to determine if it was safe to approach the house. They would use the haunting call of the bob white bird, or a shutter raised or lowered as decided, or a lit lamp in a specific window quietly gave the all clear.

They passed messages by means of moving "post offices." The post box might be a tree stump or a hollow tree. The locations changed so they didn't become known to the Yankees.

This historical marker stands in front of the public library in LaVergne, Tennessee. Photo by Betty Bolté.

Kate met John Davis during a Confederate scout gathering at her parents' house. Through her courtship with John, Kate met Sam Davis, a known Confederate spy. Kate helped Sam when he was forced to camp out in Rains Thicket near her house. She would take him a warm breakfast and hot coffee each morning that November 1863. Sam Davis was caught in Pulaski, Tennessee, and hanged as a spy on Friday, November 27, 1863.

Because John was ill with typhoid, Kate was asked to claim Sam's body and bring it back to his home. She took her nine-year-old cousin Willie Woodruff with her to request from Major General L. Harrison Rousseau the pass to go to Pulaski because "a dear aunt was nearing death and she must rush to her bedside." He gave her the pass, but tried to persuade her to wait until morning. When she reached the Duck River, the ferry had stopped for the night. She decided to cross it with her horse and buggy. She managed to encourage and steer the frightened horse through the cold waters as it swam across the river, all the while keeping her young, scared cousin calm beside her. Once they reached Pulaski, they stayed with Dr. Batts and his family. Some people say that Kate succeeded in claiming the body of Sam Davis—Smyrna, Tennessee's boy hero. Some believe that another friend of the Davis family, John Kennedy, brought Sam Davis home.

Kate married John Davis on February 25, 1864, at the Patterson farm. John was killed during an explosion on *The David White*, a steamboat he'd purchased. He died February 27, 1867 on the Mississippi River, near Helena, Arkansas. Luckily for Kate, she had not yet boarded the boat as planned. The death of her husband seemed almost more than she could bear for some time.

However, she married a Mr. Hill later. Mr. Hill is a bit of a mystery. There isn't much information known about him, other than he died an early death.

On December 30, 1884, Mary Kate Patterson Davis Hill married again, this time to Colonel Robert Kyle. They were married in Rutherford County. Colonel Kyle had served with the South during the Civil War. They moved to LaVergne to a house one-half mile from the old Nashville Highway, south of LaVergne on what today is called Fergus Road.

Colonel Kyle died at the age of 93 in their LaVergne home. He was buried in Texas, his home state. The house was sold August 12, 1919 to John G. Fergus. His son, George Gray Fergus lived in the house until his death in 1971. As of 1997, Ernestine Fergus still lived there.

Kate's grave marker. Photo by Betty Bolté.

Mary Kate Patterson Davis Hill Kyle died on Sunday, July 6, 1931. She was 93 years old. Funeral services were held for her at Trinity Methodist Church in Nashville, Tuesday morning July 8, 1931 at 10:30. She was the first woman buried in Confederate Circle in Mt. Olivet Cemetery in Nashville, Tennessee.

Check It Out!

Dunn, Marian Herndon. "Mary Kate, Heroine of LaVergne." Manuscript, 1972.

Dunn, Marian Herndon. "The Unsinkable Mary Kate." *Historical Review and Antique Digest*. Winter, 1974. Vol 3, No. 4, 14-18.

Bakeless, John. *Spies of the Confederacy*. Chapters 11-13. Philadelphia and New York: J. B. Lippincott Company, 1970.

Wait 'Til You See This!

An historical marker was erected in front of the public library in LaVergne, Tennessee, on Murfreesboro Road. It reads, in part, "Mary Kate Patterson Davis Hill Kyle, 1844-1931, Heroine of the South, worked with Coleman's Scouts and Sam Davis to spy in the LaVergne-Nolensville-Nashville area."

Kate's home in LaVergne is located just off Murfreesboro Road. When heading east, just past the public library, turn south at George Chaney Street. Go under the underpass and turn right at the grocery story onto Old Nashville Highway. Turn right again onto Fergus Road, just beyond the merge. At the end of the road sits the house. The address is 159 Fergus Street, and Ernestine Fergus (a relative of Kate's) lived there when I visited a few years ago.

Kate is buried at Mt. Olivet Cemetery in Nashville, in Confederate Circle. Her marker is flush with the ground, and located on the southwest quarter, near General Harry R. Lee, who had granted her permission to be buried here. The marker reads, "Mary Kate Patterson Davis

Hill Kyle, Sister-in-Law of Sam Davis, 1838–1931, Marker placed by Sam Davis Memorial Association & Sam Davis Chapter No 290, Order of Eastern Star."

Other Sources

Sherr, Lynn and Jurate Kazickas. *Susan B. Anthony Slept Here: A Guide to American Women's Landmarks.* 424. New York: Random House, 1994.

BELLE BOYD

1861

The Rebel Spy

Only a few days had passed since Belle's father's regiment, the 2nd Virginia Infantry, had left Martinsburg, Virginia (later called West Virginia), marching toward Harper's Ferry. Belle tried to lose herself in her books, but soon found she couldn't think about the stories knowing that her father, Ben Boyd, was heading into battle. She understood the need to fight for their freedom, but he was simply a merchant, even though he came from a long line of war veterans. She could only pray he'd come home in one piece.

She paced her room, searching her mind for something to do that she felt would help the Confederates. But what?

She knew her mother, Mary Boyd, was busy doing some task around the house. Ever since Belle's father marched out of town, her mother had become more interested in the household duties. Belle knew it was her mother's way of putting aside the cold ball of fear that she herself felt when she thought of the danger to her father. The loving face of her mother had taken on a worried expression.

MISS BELLE BOYD,
"THE REBEL SPY."

This is the earliest known image of Belle, when she was about 18 years old. Courtesy Library of Congress.

Belle had spent the last few days gathering simple extras to send to her father, items he wouldn't be able to find while on the march. Her nights, like those of her mother's, had been spent awake thinking of her father. Now she was desperate for something more to do.

Suddenly she had an idea.

"Mother!" she called, running into the kitchen. "Why can't I go see Father at the Confederate camp at Harper's Ferry? It's not that far, and there's no fighting yet. I'll go see who else wants to come along!"

Her mother watched with her mouth open as Belle hurried outside. She didn't try to stop her, knowing from experience that once 17-year-old Belle made up her mind about something, nobody could change it.

Belle gathered a group of neighbors who all had relatives and friends at the camp, and they were off for Harper's Ferry. When they arrived, the camp was alive with men in gray uniforms. Everyone was excited at the unexpected fun brought by family and friends from Martinsburg. The camp felt like a picnic ground, with much laughter. But as with all picnics, it had to end. Word spread in June that the Federal forces under General Patterson were approaching Harper's Ferry, so Colonel Thomas Jonathan Jackson took his troops out to see where they were and stop them if possible. The women and girls were abruptly sent home, back to their sad, fearful days of waiting and wondering how their boys were doing.

Early on the morning of July 3, 1861, Belle awoke to the deep boom of artillery and the sound of muskets. She jumped from her bed, no longer sleepy, and dressed. She hurried downstairs and soon learned that the Yankees were approaching the town.

Around 10 a.m., Belle watched from inside the makeshift hospital as Jackson's men passed through in full retreat. The Rebels marched quickly and proudly, trying to reach the main body of the army under General J. E. Johnston in Winchester. She watched as the rear of the column went by, protected by Turner Ashby's cavalry. She prayed they'd be safe.

Close behind them came the enemy. The Federal army paraded through the streets, cheering happily at their easy victory. The fife and drum played the marching tune. The rattle of the gun-carriages filled the street, as the cavalry rode through on gleaming horses, the plumes on top of the soldiers' hats fluttering in the wind.

While Belle was impressed by the size and condition of the Federal army, her heart sank at the sad sight of their arrival. Her hometown had been taken by the enemy.

Belle turned back to the feverish soldier lying on the cot in front of her. She had to help him, comfort him, even though he didn't know where he was or what was happening outside. Another wounded soldier lay nearby, also ill and feverish. Eliza, her maid, came into the room carrying a pile of clean rags to bathe the sweating men.

"At least Jackson removed the rest of the wounded," Belle said, wetting a rag in a basin of cool water.

Eliza had no time to respond. Heavy footsteps echoed through the hospital. Belle turned around and came face-to-face with a Yankee captain and two privates. The captain held a Federal flag, and walking over to the two feverish men, waved it over their heads and called them "—rebels."

Surprised and upset that the captain could be so ungallant with ill men, Belle said coolly, "Sir, these men are as helpless as babies, and have, as you may see, no power to reply to your insults."

"And pray," said he, "who may you be, Miss?"

She decided not to tell him who she was, but Eliza answered, "A rebel lady."

The captain sneered and immediately left, saying as he went, "a — independent one, at all events."

Belle watched as he and the two privates left the room. Then she turned to Eliza.

"These boys need a more comfortable place where they can get well."

Soon the two men were carried outside on litters. Once outside, though, Belle realized they were in even more danger, for the Yankees crowded around and threatened to stab them with their bayonets. She could smell the whiskey on their breath as they yelled insults at the helpless men. Knowing she needed help, she scanned the hate-filled faces until she discovered an officer.

"Please, sir," she cried, "help these men get to safety!"

The officer promptly calmed the men, and allowed the litters to pass without any harm. As Belle strode beside the two men, she vowed to never forget that the insults she'd just heard aimed at the two sick men could easily have been said to her father.

The next day was Independence Day, July 4, 1861. But for the people living in Martinsburg it was no longer a time of celebration, for they had separated themselves from the United States. However, the invading Yankees celebrated all day.

Belle awoke to a bright sunny day filled with the cheers and shouts of the men in the streets. The hated strains of *Yankee Doodle* drifted through the window. As the day went by, Belle heard the noise in the streets grow as the men drank more and more whiskey and started fighting among themselves and the townspeople. The officers were unable to control the men, and the soldiers began breaking into the homes. Belle heard shots fired, and found out the men were shooting through the window panes. She hoped her home would be spared by the vandals.

Her hopes were not to be.

A group of soldiers suddenly broke into the house. Belle watched in horror as the stinking, angry, loud men began taking things from throughout her home.

"I heard that young miss's room has Rebel flags all over it," one soldier said to another. Eliza, who was standing nearby, dashed upstairs to Belle's room. Belle remained quiet with an effort.

"Let's get them." The soldiers stomped their way upstairs, with Belle close behind, to Belle's room. When they entered the room, they found no flag, for Eliza had torn down the Stars and Bars and burned it before they could get there.

Belle braced herself for the next evil thing these men would dream up. One pulled out a Federal flag from somewhere.

"Let's fly this over the house, so that everyone in town will know that these women have switched to being Yankees!"

Belle's mother had stayed downstairs, but when the drunken soldiers tried to stagger their way past her, she stopped them.

"Men, every member of my household will die before that flag shall be raised over us," she said very quietly, but very firmly.

Belle, coming down the stairs, couldn't help but feel proud of her mother, and afraid for her life.

One of the soldiers stepped up to Mrs. Boyd and said words that Belle had never heard used to her mother before. She could feel her blood boil in her veins as her hatred for the Yankees swelled inside her. Almost without thinking, she drew her pistol from its hiding place, and shot the soldier.

He fell to the floor, stunning the other soldiers gathered around. Quickly they scooped him off the floor and carried him outside. Before they'd carried him far, he died.

Belle went to her mother and comforted her after the shock of seeing her daughter shoot a soldier in their own house.

"Oh, missus, missus!" a servant cried, running inside. "They're going to burn the house down; they're piling stuff up against it! Oh, if only the master was home!"

Terror spread through Belle at the idea of the house being burned down around them. She sent a message with one of her servants to the Federal officer in command. When he arrived soon thereafter, the soldiers who had caused all the trouble were arrested before being able to set on fire the material piled against the house.

The officer asked many detailed questions about what exactly happened. Finally he said to Belle, that she "had done perfectly right." He posted sentries around the house to guard it from any more problems.

Belle soon realized that having her house guarded by Yankees, with their officers coming by daily to check on their safety, made it very easy to gather information about the Federal army. She began to talk daily with the soldiers on guard. She used her feminine charm to chat freely with the sentries, then pieced together the information and wrote a note to J.E.B. Stuart and other Confederate leaders. Eliza, or another of her messengers, delivered the notes.

She hoped and prayed that she wouldn't be caught, because she knew the penalty for spying—death by hanging.

Less than a week after she shot the Yankee soldier, Belle received a guest at her house. The Third Assistant Provost-Marshal of the Federal army, Captain James Gwyn of the 23rd Pennsylvania Infantry, stood in her hallway.

"Yes, Captain?" Belle asked, puzzled.

"Miss Belle Boyd?" he asked. "I have orders to escort you to headquarters for questioning."

She soon found herself seated in the office of the angry colonel in charge.

"Miss Boyd, we have a message in your handwriting. This is a very serious offense."

Belle listened as the furious colonel threatened and scolded her for a good while. She felt no fear. She had the courage to be calm.

"I want to read to you the Article of War regarding spying, and believe me, it will be carried out to the letter if you are caught sending messages to the Rebels again."

Belle listened as he read the following:

Article of War.

Whoever shall give food, ammunition, information to, or aid and abet the enemies of the United States Government in any manner whatever, shall suffer death, or whatever penalty the honorable members of the court-martial shall see fit to inflict.

When the colonel finished his lecture, Belle stood up gracefully. "Thank you, gentlemen of the jury," she said and left.

Her heart was on fire with plans for revenge against the Yankees who felt they could control her. Little did they realize that she had been doing more than just writing notes. She'd been stealing Yankee pistols, swords, and supplies, and sending them to the Confederate camp. She had been in great danger back there, but in her heart she felt that what she did was just.

As the war continued, Belle found herself participating in various ways. For a while, she worked as a nurse at the hospital in Front Royal, Virginia, until her own health suffered and she was forced to go home to recover. Then, while visiting her father in Manassas, she received permission to be a courier between General Beauregard, General Jackson, and the officers beneath them.

The 2nd Virginia Infantry spent the winter of 1861-2 in Martinsburg. Thus, Belle was able to see her father throughout the cold months. During that time, Ben Boyd was assigned to the 7th Virginia Cavalry, under the command of Colonel Turner Ashby. As the weather warmed early in 1862, Ashby ordered his men out of Martinsburg to prepare for action.

Before leaving in March 1862, Belle's father sent her to her aunt in Front Royal, Virginia, where she would be safe. Belle knew he feared she would be captured and punished for her spying activities. She, and her maid Eliza, went without a fuss.

She briefly stayed with her aunt and uncle, James Erskine and Frances Elizabeth Stewart, at Strickler House. Once more, she enjoyed playing with her cousins, Fannie and Alice.

On March 12, however, Mr. and Mrs. Stewart and Fannie left suddenly for Richmond. Belle and Alice stayed with their grandmother, Mrs. Ruth Burns Glenn, to care for the hotel that the Stewart's had bought when they first arrived in Front Royal.

Belle Boyd. Courtesy Library of Congress, LC-BH8201-4864-A.

A battle was fought between Kimball of Shield's division and Jackson at Kernstown on March 23. When Jackson's troops lost the battle, the defeat left Front Royal open to the Yankees. The Confederates retreated up the valley.

"Alice, I hope Mother is all right. How can she be, though, with me here and Father gone? Oh, maybe I should go home."

"Belle, it's not safe. Your father wanted you away from there."

"But he didn't know this would happen. How can I leave my mother alone now?" Belle held one hand to her stomach, which was tied in knots. "I'm going home, Alice. Eliza, pack my things."

Belle and Eliza arrived in Winchester, Virginia, without any problems. The two women boarded the train to Martinsburg. As Belle looked for her seat, a Federal officer approached her.

"Good day, Miss. I am Captain Bannon. Are you Miss Belle Boyd?"

Belle raised startled eyes to the handsome face. "Yes." What on earth did he want? A Yankee officer, here, knows her name. What was next? She was glad she wasn't carrying anything important.

"I am the Assistant Provost, and I have the duty to inform you that you cannot go on until your case has been investigated; so please, get out, as the train is about to leave."

"Sir," Belle said, handing him a pass she had gotten from General Shields, "I have a pass that authorizes my maid and myself to go to Martinsburg."

The captain debated what to do. He had orders to hold her, and a pass to let her through. He decided, finally, to take her with the prisoners he was escorting to Baltimore, and deliver her to General Dix, who had ordered her held.

Belle knew there was no point in arguing, and meekly followed the captain to a seat. When the train arrived in Baltimore, she and Eliza were taken to the Eutaw House, one of the finest hotels in the city. Belle was surprised and delighted when she was visited by friends who found out she was there, as well as by people who knew her only by reputation. After a week of being held at the hotel, General Dix sent her home, unable to discover anything against her. Finally, she returned home to Martinsburg and her mother.

Martinsburg, however, was under Federal control. The Yankees did not trust Belle, and thus she was watched and never allowed to leave town. She grew restless and irritable.

"Belle, wait here," her mother said the morning of May 12. "I'm going to see what I can do."

Mrs. Boyd went to see the Provost-Marshal, Major Charles Walker of the Tenth Maine Infantry. She asked for a pass for them to go to Front Royal by way of Winchester. She had it in mind to send Belle all the way to Richmond if possible. Major Walker gave her the pass without hesitation.

When they arrived in Winchester, though, Belle was upset to find that General Shields would not allow any travel to Front Royal. But she desperately wanted to go, so she turned on her charm, and soon the local Provost Marshal, Lieutenant Colonel James S. Fillebrown of the 10th Maine Infantry, gave in and let them go.

As they approached Strickler House that evening, May 14, Belle saw that all the lights were on in the hotel.

"Mother, what is this?" she asked.

"I don't know, but I'm so hungry and tired I hope everything is all right."

Unfortunately, the hotel had become the headquarters for General Shields and his staff. They finally discovered that Alice and Grandmother Glenn were staying in the cottage in the courtyard of the large hotel.

"Mary!" cried Belle's grandmother as she hugged her daughter. "Belle! What a surprise. You must be hungry. Oh, Mary you look so tired! Sit! I'll get you some food."

Belle sank onto a chair, glad to be with family again. Welcome and warm.

Soon Belle and her mother enjoyed a home-cooked meal and told the story of how they journeyed to Front Royal.

After dinner, Belle sent her card to General Shields. She waited for a reply, and was surprised when he showed up in person to pay his respects.

"General Shields, how are you this evening?" Belle asked, trying to work him into a good mood.

"Fine, fine." The general introduced his staff officers to her.

Two of the officers were Irish. One in particular seemed to take a fancy to Belle, Captain Daniel Keily.

They chatted for a while, exchanging small talk. Finally, Belle gathered the courage to ask for a pass to go to Richmond, Virginia.

"I don't dare give you to Jackson's army when they are so demoralized at the present. But rest easy, they will soon be removed and you may go wherever you want."

Belle realized the general was acting very confident of a victory soon. He was speaking of things he shouldn't be telling anyone. Belle knew she could make good use of his words.

Before long General Shields and his two officers left the cottage. Belle wrapped her shawl about her and followed them, but not too closely. She followed them into the hotel and saw them go into the drawing room. Suddenly, she remembered a way she could hear what they said at this Council of War, and hurried upstairs to a bedroom that contained several small closets. In one of the closets, there was a hole cut into the floor. She put her ear to the small hole, and listened to the conversation below until one o'clock in the morning. During that long span of time, she wanted to stretch and stand, but she didn't dare make any noise. She wanted to hear what they were planning, and she didn't want them to know she was listening.

After the men left the room, she hurried back to the cottage and dashed off a note in code (cipher) about all that she had overheard. She considered waking Eliza and sending the note with her, but then realized it would be quieter to go herself. She slipped into her pocket a few passes she'd gotten from paroled Confederate soldiers who were heading south, just in case she was stopped. Then she raced to the stables, saddled her horse, and rode toward the mountains.

Belle must hurry to get the news to Colonel Ashby. She rode through the darkness, being stopped at several sentry posts along the way. A quick look at the pass was all she needed for them to let her through.

Once past the sentries, she rode the rest of the fifteen miles across fields, along roads, through marshes, until she reached the home of Mr. M., a friend of the family.

She jumped from her horse and ran up the steps to bang on the door until the house echoed inside. Belle knocked again, louder, praying all the while that he would hurry.

"Who's there?" someone called from a window on the second floor.

"It is I."

"But what is your name?"

"Belle Boyd. I have important information for Colonel Ashby: is he here?"

"No; but I will come down."

Belle waited impatiently. The door swung open and Mrs. M. pulled her inside. Belle told her she must find Colonel Ashby and tell him some news. Mrs. M. told her that the colonel was a quarter mile farther up in the wood. Belle thanked her and went back outside to ride on. She had raised her foot to mount the horse, when a door beside her opened and out stepped Colonel Ashby. She turned from her horse and stepped forward.

"Good God! Miss Belle, is this you? Where did you come from? Have you dropped from the clouds? Or am I dreaming?"

Belle explained how she had ridden across the fields to tell him about what she'd heard from her hiding place in the closet. She handed him the coded message, then mounted her horse and rode back toward the hotel.

She rode easily past many of the sleeping sentries. The last one, however, awoke as she galloped past. As she rode around a sharp turn, she looked back to see him aiming his pistol at her. Two hours later she was back at the hotel. She took care of her horse and went to bed as the sun rose above the horizon.

Author's Note: Belle Boyd did a great deal to aid the Rebels during the Civil War. She is known as "La Belle Rebel" for her spying and smuggling. She was arrested and jailed several times. She risked her life for her beliefs. Her story has been written many times in much greater detail than this book allows. Please see the "Check It Out!" section for more books on her life and activities.

Just the Facts

Isabelle Boyd was born on May 9, 1844, in Martinsburg, Virginia, probably at the house of her grandmother, Mrs. Samuel Boyd. She was named Isabelle in honor of one of her great-aunts. Her parents were Benjamin Reed and Mary Rebecca Glenn Boyd.

Belle spent her first years in a nearby town called Bunker Hill, where she lived in a two-storied house. The house was overgrown by roses and honeysuckle and was surrounded by silver maple trees. Her favorite activities were riding horseback through the Shenandoah Valley and exploring it on foot, hobbies that helped her in her spying.

Ben and Mary Boyd had a total of eight children. Sadly, two girls and two boys died while babies and were buried in Green Hill Cemetery in Martinsburg. Then came Isabelle, William, Glenn, and Mary.

Sometime between 1849 and 1854, Mr. Boyd built a general store on Queen Street in Martinsburg. He moved his family to a house at 126 East Burke Street, Martinsburg. When the American Civil War started, he enlisted in the Confederate States Army, with the 2nd Virginia Infantry.

When Belle was 12, in 1856, she enrolled in a finishing school at the Mount Washington Female College in Baltimore, Maryland. She studied French, classical literature, music, and singing. During her schooling, Belle's family moved from the house on East Burke to a house at 501 South Queen Street. She graduated at the age of 16, in 1860. That year she also was presented to society in Washington, D.C., not realizing that the war was fast approaching.

While attending Mount Washington, she wrote a letter to her cousin, "Master Willie Boy" in St. Joseph, Missouri, in which she describes herself:

My dearest Willie,...You would scarcely know me....I am tall....I weigh 106-1/2 pounds. My form is beautiful. My eyes are of a dark blue and so expressive. My hair of a rich brown and I think I tie it up nicely. My neck and arms are beautiful & [my] foot is per-fect....My teeth the same pearly whiteness, I think perhaps a little whiter. Nose quite as large as ever and indeed I am decidedly the most beautiful of all your cousins....I am nearly crazzy [sic] to come out west...to hunt a husband. Please tell me the names of some young gentlemen where you are and recommend me to some nice young fellow.

In Louis Sigaud's *Belle Boyd Confederate Spy*, she is described as "Vivacious in manner, in mood she could be gentle or furious, persuasive or commanding, beguiling or demanding, and she knew with unerring feminine discernment which would best serve her needs."

No one would say that Belle was modest. In fact, she made no secret of the fact that she used her womanly charms to learn secrets about the enemy position. Sometimes she was arrested, but she oftened managed to get out of trouble as easily as she got into it.

After being betrayed by a lover, she was captured on July 29, 1862 and put into the Old Capitol Prison in Washington, D.C., for one month. Then she was exchanged for Yankee prisoners held by the Rebels, and was exiled. She was arrested again in June 1863 while visiting in Martinsburg. She came down with typhoid, and was released from prison on December 1, 1863, and sent to Europe to get well. The ship she attempted to return on was captured and she met and fell in love with the prize master, Samuel Wylde Hardinge. They were married on August 25, 1864, at St. James's Church, Piccadilly, England. Belle was 20 years old.

Samuel Hardinge had some business to take care of back in the United States. He left for Boston and New York on August 26, 1864. He stopped to see Belle's parents in Martinsburg, then went to Baltimore. When he arrived at Monocacy Station, he was arrested as a deserter from the U.S. Navy. He was held at Forrest Hall prison in Washington, D.C., the worst of the Federal prisons. While there, the horrible conditions weakened him physically and mentally. He was then sent to Fort Delaware to an even harsher prison. Finally he was released on February 3, 1865, barely able to stand. He apparently sailed for London on February 8, 1865. He may have arrived there late February or early March. The record is unclear as to what exactly happened to him, but he never rejoined his bride.

Belle began a stage career while in London, in order to pay her debts. She also wrote and published her autobiography, *Belle Boyd in Camp and Prison.* She and her infant daughter Grace returned to the United States in the fall of 1866 and continued to perform.

She married Colonel John Swainton Hammond in March 1869. After only a year, her health again failed her, and she went with her husband and daughter to California. Just before a son was born to her, she had a mental breakdown. She spent six months at a mental hospital in Stockton, California, where her boy was buried. She had three more children with Hammond, but her love for him died. She divorced him on November 1, 1884.

She married Nat High less than six weeks after her divorce from Hammond. He was a struggling actor when they met. Belle was forced to go back to the stage because of money problems. Nat became her manager and they toured the country together.

Belle died June 11, 1900 from a sudden heart attack while preparing for a performance in Kilbourn (now Wisconsin Dells), Wisconsin. She was 56 years old. She had been ill for several days. When Nat High arrived, he immediately sent out a telegram to Belle's children: Grace Hardinge Bennett, Byrd Hammond, Marie Isabelle Hammond, and John Edmund Hammond. The telegram, according to Louis Sigaud's *Belle Boyd Confederate Spy*, read:

Miss Isabelle Hammond,
Groveland Avenue, Chicago, Ill.
"Mama died suddenly tonight. Come by Wednesday.

Rue High.

The funeral was held on June 13, 1900 at the Episcopal Church. She was buried at Kilbourn Cemetery, now Spring Grove Cemetery. Her tombstone says simply:

BELLE BOYD
Confederate Spy
Born in Virginia
Died in Wisconsin

_____

Erected by a Comrade

In 1976, her famous plea, "One God, one flag, one people–forever," was written on a plaque and placed near her tombstone.

Check It Out!

Fiction

Kane, Harnett T. *The Smiling Rebel.* Garden City: Doubleday & Co., Inc., 1955.

Morris, Gilbert. *Blockade Runner.* Chicago: Moody Press, 1996. (Juvenile fiction)

Nolan, Jeannette Covert. *Belle Boyd, Secret Agent.* New York: Messner, 1967. (Juvenile fiction)

Nonfiction

Bakeless, John. *Spies of the Confederacy.* "Belle Boyd" in two parts, chapters 8 and 9. Philadelphia and NY: J. B. Lippincott Company, 1970.

Boyd, Belle. *Belle Boyd in Camp and Prison.* New York: Blelock & Co., 1865 and 1867.

Kane, Harnett T. *Spies for the Blue and Gray.* "Cleopatra of the Secession." Chapter 6. Garden City: Hanover House, 1954.

Leech, Margaret. *Reveille in Washington.* New York: Harper & Bros., 1941.

Lockett, Myrta, ed. *A Virginia Girl in the Civil War, 1861-65.* New York: D. Appleton & Co., 1903.

Scarborough, Ruth. *Belle Boyd: Siren of the South.* Macon: Mercer University Press, 1983.

Sigaud, Louis A. *Belle Boyd, Confederate Spy.* Richmond: The Dietz Press, Inc., 1945. Second Edition.

Turner, Lewis McKenzie. *Belle Boyd, The Rebel Spy.* Baltimore: Salt House Press, 1928(?).

Wood, Leonard W. *Belle Boyd, Famous Spy of the Confederate States Army.* Keyser: The Mountain Echo, 1940.

Wait 'Til You See This!

The house that Belle's father, Benjamin Boyd, built in Martinsburg is now the site of the Berkeley County Historical Society. The address is 126 E. Race Street, Martinsburg, West Virginia. The original house on South Queen Street is marked by a plaque.

Belle's grave is located at Spring Grove Cemetery, Route 23, Wisconsin Dells, Wisconsin.

The Arlington National Cemetery now houses a memorial to women veterans, where you can learn more about Belle Boyd and others through a computer database of personal stories, artifacts, pictures, and histories.

The Old Capitol Prison was located at First Street and Maryland Avenue NE in Washington, D.C. It was torn down in 1867. Three buildings were built in its place, called Trumbull Row and served as the headquarters for the National Woman's Party until 1929. Today, you will see the Supreme Court, which was built in the 1930s.

The Shenandoah Valley Warren Rifles Confederate Museum is maintained by the United Daughters of the Confederacy. It houses flags, weapons, uniforms, and letters from the Civil War. You can see an autographed photo of Belle Boyd. The museum is located at 95 Chester Street, Warren, Virginia, and is open April 15 through November 1, or by appointment, Mon-Sat 9-5, Sun 1-5.

Other Sources

Atlanta Journal and Constitution. "Southern Digest Girl Scouts' Honor." March 1, 1992. Dixie Living Section, M, 3. The Atlanta Constitution, 1992.

Belle Boyd Birthday Celebration notice. *Washington Times.* May 20, 1995.

Boltz, Martha M. "Legacies of the Daughters of the Confederacy." *The Washington Times*, November 5, 1994. Part B, B3. News World Communications Inc., 1994.

Charleston Gazette. "Belle Boyd's Birthday Celebration." May 18, 1995.

Conroy, Sarah Booth. "Notes from Washington's Underground." *The Washington Post.* April 26, 1992, Style Section, F1, Chronicles.

Jones, Katharine M. *Heroines of Dixie.* The Bobbs-Merrill Co., Inc., 1955. 172-5, 254-8.

"Military Museums." *Washington Post.* June 6, 1986, Weekend Section, 22.

News Wire Services. "Memorial to Pay Belated Tribute to Women Who Served in the Armed Forces." *The Buffalo News.* June 23, 1995, News Section, 3A.

Rable, George C. *Civil Wars: Women and the Crisis of Southern Nationalism.* 136-153. Board of Trustees of the University of Illinois. Champaign: University of Illinois Press, 1989.

Robertson, James I. Jr. "Spy, Actress, Fugitive—Boyd was Belle of Confederacy." *The Washington Times.* April 18, 1992, Part B, Life Section, B3. News World Communications, Inc., 1992.

Ross, Nancy L. "Funds Sought to Save Civil War Spy's Home." *The Washington Post.* August 6, 1992. Home Section, T5, Home Front.

Scruggs, Afi-Odelia E. "Troupe Brings Women Onstage: It Dusts Off History Books to Dramatize Lives." *The Plain Dealer.* July 7, 1994. Metro Section, 1B. Plain Dealer Publishing Co., 1994.

Sherr, Lynn and Jurate Kazickas. *Susan B. Anthony Slept Here: A Guide to American Women's Landmarks.* 460, 484, 498-9. New York: Random House, 1994.

Sifakis, Stewart. *Who Was Who in the Civil War.* 65-6. New York: Facts on File, Inc., 1988.

Simmons, Jeff. "Making History Her Story: Englewood Author Focuses on Women Who Made a Difference." *The Record.* July 8, 1992, Northern Valley Section, 1. Bergen Record Corp, 1992.

Slater, Thomas. "Belle Meets Stonewall—Or so the Story Goes." *The Washington Times*, May 6, 1995. Part B, B3. News World Communications Inc., 1995.

Sullivan, Walter, ed. *The War the Women Loved: Female Voices from the Confederate South*. 113-190, 310. Nashville: J.S. Sanders & Company, 1995.

Swindle, Kathy. "Bureau with a Past: A Notorious Confederate Spy Once Owned This Chest of Drawers." *The Dallas Morning News*. March 26, 1993, House and Garden Section, 10G.

"Watch Your Step! Who Knows What Once Went on Right Where You're Standing?" Excerpts from "On This Spot." *Roll Call*. April 23, 1992, Constituent's Guide Section. Levitt Communications, Inc., 1992.

Wiley, Bell Irvin. *Confederate Women*. 143. Westport: Greenwood Press, 1975.

NANCY CROUSE

1862

In the Face of Danger

Nancy awoke early on the morning of September 10, 1862. She rubbed the sleep from her eyes, listening to the murmur of conversation coming through the walls, then slipped out of bed. Somehow the very air seemed different this morning. She poured water from the pitcher into the basin, and splashed her face. The cold water tingled, taking away any desire to stay abed. She stopped at the window and peered at the street running through her hometown of Middletown, Maryland. Situated near South Mountain, the city fell away downhill to her left and rose to the right. A white church stood directly across from her house, nestled between other two-story clapboards like her own. She loved this town, and its people. Her thoughts strayed to one boy she'd seen recently. His name was John Bennett. She'd like to get to know him better.

The clatter of shoes and the high voices of younger children echoed down the stairs, announcing her three sisters and brother heading to breakfast.

"Nancy, time for breakfast," her mother said, passing her door.

"Coming!" Nancy yelled, then made a face. She tried so very hard to be ladylike, but she couldn't seem to control her impulses. Yelling was simply not done in the Crouse household.

She dressed and raced down the long flight of stairs to the dining room. She didn't stop to hang the flag out as normal. Her mother would not be pleased if she delayed, but right after breakfast it would fly boldly where the approaching Rebel troops could see it. If they were still coming.

Her long skirts swirled about her ankles as she stopped suddenly to avoid running into her mother.

"Nancy, how many times must I remind you that you are a young lady of 17 years now, and young ladies do *not* run down the stairs."

Nancy bowed her head, and bobbed a curtsey. "Yes, mother." She followed her mother into the kitchen. To herself she wished she was 14 again like her sister Martha, or even nine like Rebecca. And of course Charles, at eight, was allowed to do whatever he wanted to, almost more so than little Frances as she changed from being a toddler to a little girl of five. Sometimes, Nancy thought, it was better to be a kid.

"Please take your seat and we'll eat breakfast." Mother had already taken her place, her napkin laying neatly across her lap.

Nancy sighed and sat down, a bit too fast for a lady. Growing up was so hard. Nancy don't run. Nancy walk slowly. Nancy don't yell. So many rules about what she could and could not do, how did anyone remember all of them? Would any man be interested in her if she couldn't learn them? She ate her toast and fried eggs as quietly as possible, being careful not to slurp her tea.

Martha ate silently beside her, missing her father. Nancy snuck a peek at the thin features of Malinda, her brother George's wife. She didn't blame Malinda for joining them for breakfast each morning. Her nearby house must be lonely. There was no sound from out back of her father and brother, both saddle makers, tanning the leather, or driving rivets into the glossy surface. Nancy could only imagine how much Malinda missed her husband; almost as much as Nancy missed her father. Rebecca, Charles and Frances, along with Nancy's cousins Flowena, five, and Martin, four, chattered amongst themselves, arguing about what they would play outside after they finished eating.

"Mother?"

"Yes, Nancy?"

"Any word on the war? Where are the troops? Are they coming this way like everyone has been saying?" Nancy asked. Malinda drew in a sharp breath, but continued to stare at her plate.

A growing movement to stop slavery had seen Abraham Lincoln elected president of the United States. Together with the debate over whether the new territories should allow slavery, the issue had become a hot argument across the country. The southern states who wanted to keep slavery broke away from the Union and began taking over U.S. government property, which led to the beginning of the Civil War on April 11, 1861 at Ft. Sumter, in Charleston, South Carolina. Often brothers fought against, and killed, brothers. The Crouse family believed in the unity of the country, thus they were Unionists. Nancy's father, George W. Crouse, and her brother, George, were off fighting for that belief.

"I've heard General Robert E. Lee ordered his troops to Frederick a few days ago. We'll probably see those Rebels pass right down our fair main street again."

"Right through town?" Nancy cried in horror. "Not again–surely they'll go around us, leave us alone!" She remembered vividly when the churches right here in Middletown had been full of soldiers wounded during a skirmish on May 24, 1862. The 1st Maryland Cavalry had fought bravely during that battle, but it was terrifying to hear the guns fired, the cannons booming, the screams of men in torture, all through the day. She hoped none of her classmates would be hurt or killed in battle, but she knew they were fighting for a worthy cause—freedom.

"Nancy, mind your tone," Ellen Crouse replied.

"Mother, I can't be calm when we've got those dirty Rebels coming right past our house! And with Father and George gone this time, too."

"The troops may be here today or tomorrow, Nancy. You'll have time to beat the rugs and sweep the porch," Mrs. Crouse added, "then stay inside until they've passed. Same for the rest of you—stay inside."

"Yes, Mother."

"Yes, Ma'am," the younger children echoed.

Martha set her tea cup down and said, "At least that Rebel hussy, Belle Boyd, has been captured and is behind bars, right where she should be."

"No, she's been freed. Hadn't you heard?" Malinda said, meeting Martha's eye.

"To start spying against us again!" Nancy cried. Secretly she had mixed feelings about Belle Boyd. She was just a little older than herself, and she believed in her side's cause as fiercely as Nancy believed in the Union.

Nancy Crouse's house in Middletown, Maryland. Photo by Betty Bolté.

"They let her go back to Dixie," Malinda added. "I hear she's in Richmond now."

"Well, let's hope she stays there and behaves as a young lady should," Mrs. Crouse said. She slid gracefully from her chair. "The sun is climbing and we each have work to do."

Nancy cleared the breakfast dishes and washed them up, while Martha straightened away the mess from preparing the meal. Rebecca picked up the braided rugs from the hallway and parlor and took them out behind the house so Nancy could beat them. With each swing, dust billowed into the air. Nancy pictured the Rebels with their gray uniforms, and swung harder, taking out her anger over slavery on the defenseless rugs. Once cleaned thoroughly, she carried them back inside and laid them out.

Suddenly she thought of the United States flag waiting to be hung outside. She raced up the stairs, gathered it into her arms, and carried it to the front bedroom, where she hung it on the pole out the window. She watched the 34 stars on the blue background dance with the 13 red and white stripes, and sighed. The flag symbolized freedom for everyone who lived in the country, not just those of a particular skin color. On July 22, 1862, President Abraham Lincoln had declared that the slaves must be set free, and that had fueled the war even more. She hoped that it would end quickly and Papa and George would come home safe.

She turned and went back downstairs. Taking up the broom, she headed for the front porch. Charles thundered down the hall towards her, a frantic Frances chasing him, clutching a headless cornhusk doll in her hand. Nancy chuckled and moved aside to let them pass.

As she stepped onto the porch, her friend Effie Titlow walked up the few steps from the street to the wooden planks.

"Morning, Nancy," Effie said.

"Morning, Effie. What brings you out so early?" Nancy set aside the broom as she talked with her friend. She recalled her mother telling her that a lady didn't do household chores when entertaining company.

"I thought you'd like to know—an advance detachment from the Confederate cavalry is heading this way. They're close by!"

"Are those rascals coming into town?" Nancy asked, her eyes darting up the street.

Effie nodded. "They aren't far away at all. You should take that flag down before it gets you in trouble."

Nancy gazed at the flag, stirring peacefully in the crisp fall breeze. A deep blue sky provided a perfect background for the Stars and Stripes. She thought about what the flag stood for, what her family believed, why the men were fighting. She turned back to Effie with a determined smile. "No. It stays right there."

Effie shrugged. "Don't say I didn't warn you."

A clatter and rumble from down the hill to the west caught the young ladies' attention. In the distance they could see a cloud rising along the street as the Confederate cavalry rode into town.

"There they are!" cried Nancy. "I hope our troops come soon and catch them."

The riders approached purposefully, heading for the next town of Frederick to meet up with the rest of the Confederate soldiers. As Nancy and Effie watched them from the narrow porch, the cavalrymen suddenly saw the United States flag hanging above the ladies' heads. The detachment stopped and several men dismounted.

Nancy watched with defiant horror as they ran up onto the porch. They were dirty, smelly, and had holes and tears throughout their uniforms. The set of their jaws and the glint in their eyes sent a shiver through her. She could see Effie shaking with fear as she backed against the house. Nancy raised her chin. This was her house and they had no right to be on her porch without an invitation.

"Give me that damn Yankee rag!" one officer demanded.

"No." Nancy said it as calmly as she could, but she thought she heard her voice waver. She bristled at his attitude and language.

"While this town is occupied by Confederate forces, the town will fly the Stars and Bars!" the officer snapped. He made for the door, but Nancy was quicker.

"You'll never take my flag from me!" She dashed inside and scrambled up the steps to the front bedroom window. Snatching the flag from its post, she held it around herself and came back downstairs. Her mother stopped her for a moment, about to say something, then released her arm. Nancy saw her brother and sisters, Malinda and her children, gathered behind her mother, eyes wide and glistening.

"They won't hurt me," Nancy said. "They wouldn't dare."

"I hope you're right," her mother said.

Nancy stepped onto the front porch, sure that wearing the flag would end the matter. No gentleman would harm her in her own home.

The officer grew even angrier at her display of Union pride. "Girl, give me that damned Yankee rag, right now."

"Not as long as I live." Nancy tucked the flag closer around her body. She heard Effie inhale sharply and noticed the revolver in the officer's hand. He placed the muzzle of the gun to her head and growled, "Divest yourself of those colors."

"You may shoot me, but never will I willingly give up my country's flag into the hands of traitors," Nancy declared.

"You'll give me that flag, or I'll take it." The officer pushed the muzzle into her skin, hurting her. "Off your dead body, if necessary."

Nancy realized she couldn't win. There were too many cavalrymen around, all looking like they would follow this officer's orders without hesitation. She released her grip on the flag and the officer grabbed it from her. The troops cheered at their minor victory. Within moments the men remounted, the officer tied the flag around his horse's head, and the detachment galloped up the hill, bound for Frederick.

"Oh, Nancy, I don't know whether that was the bravest or stupidest thing I've ever seen," Effie exclaimed, sinking to the floor.

Nancy put her hand to her heart. "They stole my flag." Tears rolled down her cheeks. "Those traitors put their grubby hands all over my beautiful flag—they had no right, Effie."

"I am just glad that is over."

The door opened behind them, and everyone crowded onto the porch.

"You were very brave, daughter," Mrs. Crouse said, giving her shoulders a squeeze.

"But they stole my flag!" Nancy cried.

"Nancy, look!" Effie said. She was pointing downhill at a second cloud of dust approaching. Soon another detachment of cavalry rode into view, this time Union cavalrymen. Without pausing to think, Nancy dashed into the street waving her arms. "Captain! Captain!"

The riders halted at her distressed cries.

"Captain, the Rebels have stolen our country's flag from me!"

"How long ago, Miss?" the captain asked.

"Just a few minutes. Please, if you can, bring it back to me?"

"My pleasure, but we have to catch them first." The detachment spurred their horses and galloped up the hill, hot on the heels of the Rebel detachment.

"Nancy, Effie, come inside and have something to drink. There's no reason to stand out here and put yourselves in any more danger," Mrs. Crouse said, ushering everyone inside.

Reluctantly, Nancy followed Effie into the coolness of the clapboard house. She sat at the kitchen table with her mother and friend, her family surrounding her and talking all at once, and tried not to think about the flag. The conversation turned to other everyday topics, but Nancy didn't hear what they were saying. A short time later a sharp rap on the front door caused Nancy to leap from her chair.

"Nancy! Please." Mrs. Crouse took her arm and slowed her down as they made their way to answer the door. The Union Captain waited, hat in hand, on the other side.

"Madame, Miss," he said, nodding respectfully. "We have recovered something which I believe belongs to you?" He smiled as a second officer produced Nancy's beloved flag, a little dirty but still in one glorious piece.

Nancy pushed open the door and took it from the officer. "Thank you ever so much, sir!" she cried. "How did you manage to bring it back so quickly?"

"We caught up with those Rebs and we captured them, all except their captain who got away from us."

"Well done, sir," Mrs. Crouse said, her arm around Nancy's shoulders.

"Excuse me, Captain. I must hang our flag again."

"Of course. Good-day ladies."

Nancy ran up the stairs uncaring of her mother's reproachful look, and into the front bedroom, where she once again hung the flag proudly on its pole. She stood back and admired it, glad to see it back in its proper place.

Just the Facts

Nancy Crouse was born in 1844 somewhere in Illinois. Her father, George W. Crouse, was a saddler by trade. The census records indicate that George W. was married to a woman named Ellen in 1850, but by 1860 his wife is listed as Catharine. Apparently something happened to Nancy's mother between the two censuses. Additionally, Nancy had several brothers and sisters: George, born 1834; Mary, born 1836; Phoebe, born 1839; Catharine, born 1840; Laura, born 1843; Martha, born 1848; Rebecca, born 1852; Charles, born 1853; and Frances, born 1856.

Most of the preceding account was fiction, however the facts behind the story are based on evidence. The story as told by George C. Rhoderick, Jr. includes several quotes that are included in the above story. In particular, the Confederate cavalryman did ask for "that damned Yankee rag" and Nancy reportedly replied as quoted. All other dialogue was written to enhance the telling of the story.

Nancy married John H. Bennett, of Frederick. She died in Frederick on February 22, 1908, but the spirit in which she lived her life continues throughout Maryland.

Nancy's Ballad

Thomas Chalmers Harbaugh wrote a ballad in honor of Nancy's bravery. He changed the story a bit to make it more poetic.

> You've heard the story of Nancy Crouse,
> > The Valley maid, who stood one day
> Beneath the porch of her humble house,
> > And boldly defied the men in gray;
> Over Catoctin's lengthening ridge,
> > Out from many a bosky glen,
> Down the pick and over the bridge,
> > Booted and spurred, rode Stonewall's men.
>
> Under the spires of Middletown,
> > Glinted many a rebel gun;
> The dear old flag, they said, must down,
> > Nor flaunt its folds in Autumn's sun;
> Mighty legions, clad in gray,
> > Cursed the banner of the stars,
> And o'er the hills and far away,
> > Streamed the standards of the bars.
>
> Nancy Crouse looked out and saw
> > The old flag floating on the breeze,
> Emblem fair of truth and law;
> > Then as suddenly, she sees
> Foam-flecked steed and rider stern
> > Who the standard has espied;
> With an oath his hot lips burn,
> > For the flag he turns aside.

From the house the maiden springs
      Grips the flag and round her form
Wraps it, while the cool air rings
      With the portent of the storm;
With an oath the wretch in gray
      Tries away the flag to tear,
Whilst the girl's eyes seem to say;
      Bold, defiant: "If you dare!"

Closer to her form she clasps
      The beauteous flag our fathers gave,
And the rebel's oaths and gasps
      Threaten her with early grave;
"Not for you!" her words rang true,
      "Not for you this banner fair,
You wear gray, its friends wear blue;
      It was blessed with many a pray'r."

With a final curse and threat,
      Rides the rebel far away.
And the flag once more is set
      O'er the porch to taunt the Gray;
Smiling, Nancy sees the horde
      Vanish down the village street;
Gleaming gun and swirling sword,
      Once more in the distance meet.

Honor to the Maryland maid,
      Who the banner saved that day
When thro' Autumn sun and shade
      Marched the legions of the Gray;

Middletown remembers yet
        How the tide of war was stay'd,
And the years will not forget
        Nancy Crouse, the Valley Maid.

Gone are Stonewall's legions true,
        Battle drums have ceased to beat,
And the Banners of the Blue
        Wave not in the village street;
But the years on Nancy brave,
        Will of praise bestow the meed;
Time for her will honor crave,
        And the world will hail her deed!

The Ballad of Nancy Crouse is taken from *Middletown Valley in Song and Story*, 1910, by T. C. Harbaugh. Used by permission.

Check It Out!

Adams, Charles S. *The Civil War in Frederick County Maryland: A Guide to 49 Historic Points of Interest.* Published 1996 by Charles S. Adams, 201 Ryan Ct., Shepherdstown, WV 25443.

Rhoderick, George C. Jr. *The Early History of Middletown Maryland.* Published by the Middletown Valley Historical Society.

Wait 'Til You See This!

The Nancy Crouse House stands at 204 Main Street, Middletown, Maryland.

Other Sources

Census records for the Middletown Election District in the County of Frederick, in the State of Maryland, taken 1850 and 1860.

Sherr, Lynn and Jurate Kazickas. *Susan B. Anthony Slept Here: A Guide to American Women's Landmarks*. 191. New York: Random House, 1994.

EMMA SANSOM

1863

Crossing Black Creek

Emma saw movement out the window over the kitchen sink. She paused in washing the breakfast dishes as she saw mounted Yankee soldiers ride into view. Drying her hands, she called to her mother Lamila, and her sister Jennie. She grabbed her blue bonnet with white polka dots and tied it on her head. She liked the way it complemented her blue cotton dress. They ran outside to watch the company of men wearing dark blue uniforms ride past on mules and horses. She soon learned they were part of Colonel Abel Streight's command.

"They're heading for the bridge across Black Creek," Emma's mother said.

"Look, Ma, there's more coming," Emma cried. She tucked a strand of auburn hair back behind an ear as she watched the men marching toward them.

A large group of soldiers stopped at the front gate. They scanned the plain one-story farmhouse. The house overlooked Black Creek and was surrounded by a post-and-rail fence. Stately trees surrounded the house, and a dirt road ran in front of it. There were no slave quarters as the Sansom's only ever had one slave, Aunt Fannie, who had raised the 12 children over the years.

"Morning, ladies," said one of the soldiers. "Can you bring us some water?"

Emma and Jennie grabbed buckets and filled them, trying to hurry them on their way. Emma could only hope the soldiers would move along without taking anything more. Her mother had given all they could spare to the Confederate army and now they were barely surviving from their small farm. At one time the farm had supported the 14 members of the family and Aunt Fannie. Now only Emma, Jennie, and their mother lived there. They believed in their right to live as free as they were born, and under whatever form of government was voted best. They had sacrificed for the Cause and for her only brother who was serving in the Rebel army.

This photo of Emma was taken after the war. From Life of General Nathan Bedford Forrest. *Used by permission.*

She gave her bucket to a dusty soldier near the gate.

"Where's your father?" he asked her as he sipped the cool water.

"He's dead," Emma replied, looking him square in the eye. She wouldn't let him know how distraught they'd been when her dad died Christmas eve just 18 months before.

"Do you have any brothers?"

"I have six brothers," she said, continuing to look at him. He didn't need to know they weren't here at the moment.

"Do they think the South will win?" the soldier asked.

"They do."

"What do you think about it?"

"I think God is on our side and we will win," Emma replied confidently, despite being only 16 years old.

"You do?" the soldier asked, shaking his head. "Well, if you had seen us whip Colonel Roddey the other day and run him across the Tennessee River, you would have thought God was on the side of the best artillery."

Emma noticed the men beginning to dismount their somewhat rested horses and mules.

"Let's go inside," her mother said, ushering the two girls into the house.

The soldiers followed the women, however, and began to search for guns and rifles, and men's saddles. Emma watched as they went through all their belongings, careless of what they touched. She stifled a cry as they found her sidesaddle and cut the skirts off of it.

"You men bring a chunk of fire with you, and get out of that house!" The order came from a man outside.

The soldiers snatched some fire from the fireplace and left the house. An officer posted a guard around the farmhouse "for their protection." Emma suspected that it was because she and her family were sympathetic with the Southern fight. The soldiers headed for the bridge crossing Black Creek and before long smoke rose from the wooden planks, burning the only way across the river.

Emma's mother suddenly remembered their fence extended to the railing of the bridge and she hurried outside.

"Come with me," she said, "and we'll pull our rails away, so they will not be destroyed."

The girls followed their mother to the top of the hill, but they were too late. The rails had been piled on the bridge and were burning. The Yankees stood to one side, guarding it.

The Emma Sansom Monument in Gadsden, Alabama shows Emma guiding General Forrest. Photo by Betty Bolté.

Emma started back to the house, her steps slow. Her mother and sister came behind her. Suddenly Emma saw a Yankee running toward her, being chased by Rebel soldiers.

"Halt! Surrender!" the Rebels shouted.

The Yankee threw up his hand and stopped. He handed over his gun to an officer.

"Ladies," that officer said, "do not be alarmed. I am General Forrest. I and my men will protect you."

Emma recognized General Nathan Bedford Forrest sitting on his horse, looking determined and confident despite the tiredness at the edges of his eyes. She could tell from the condition of the soldiers and their horses that they'd been fighting long and hard, and she knew they weren't done yet.

"Where are the Yankees?" General Forrest asked.

"They have set the bridge on fire and are standing in a line on the other side," Emma's mother replied. "If you go down there, they will kill all of you."

As more of the Rebel soldiers appeared, shooting began across the river. "Inside!" Emma's mother shouted.

Emma, her mother, and her sister raced toward the house. Emma's blue bonnet slipped off her head and onto her back with each step. She arrived first inside the fence gate, where she paused to glance back.

General Forrest galloped up to the gate and asked her, "Can you tell me where I can get across the creek?"

"There's another bridge two miles down river, but it's not safe," Emma replied. "There's also a way to cross that the cows use in low water, and it's only a few hundred yards from here. Your men should be able to cross there. Saddle my horse, and I'll show you."

"There's no time for that. Ride here behind me," General Forrest said.

He moved his horse near the bank and Emma jumped on behind him and the horse stepped forward.

"Emma, where are you going?" Emma's mother cried.

"She is showing me where to cross the creek," General Forrest said. "Then my men can catch the Yankees before they get to Rome. Don't worry; I will bring her back."

With that, he kicked the horse and they rode away. Emma showed him where to ride across a field with a deep ravine and undergrowth that protected them from view across the river. As they approached the creek, she told him they should dismount so they wouldn't be seen. He agreed and they dismounted.

Emma guided him through some bushes until they reached the edge of the ford. Emma peered up and down the river, saying that she'd go first because the Yanks wouldn't dare shoot her. Suddenly General Forrest stepped in front of her.

"I am glad to have you for a pilot, but I am not going to make a breastworks of you."

Emma heard the cannon being fired time and again, too fast to count. Stopping by a black gum tree, she pointed out where to go into the water and where to get out on the other side.

"Thank you, young miss. Now let's get you back safe, as I promised your ma," General Forrest said, turning back toward the house.

Emma followed him back through the bushes to his horse.

"What is your name?" General Forrest asked.

"Emma Sansom," she replied.

"May I have a lock of your hair, for luck and to remember you by?" he asked.

"Certainly, sir."

Forrest entrusted Emma's safe return to Sargeant William Williams, who proudly returned her to her house.

Forrest led his men across the creek using the path Emma had just shown him. Cannon balls screamed over their heads. Emma covered her ears at the loud noise.

"Ladies, you should take cover somewhere away from here," Williams said.

They didn't need to be told twice. Emma, Jennie, and their mother ran for cover in the forest. Once the fighting stopped, they went back to the house. Along the way, they passed General Forrest again.

"Miss Sansom, I've written a note for you. You'll find it on your bureau. And I'd still like a lock of your hair, if I may have one?"

"Certainly, sir."

"One of my bravest men has been killed, and he is laid out in the house. His name is Robert Turner. Will you see that he is buried in some graveyard near here?"

Emma felt honored to be entrusted with such a duty. To bury a man who had died fighting for her family's personal rights was a privilege.

She gave General Forrest the lock of hair he'd asked for, then he said good-bye and the Rebels continued their pursuit of Streight.

Emma smiled at Jennie, and they went into the parlor where the soldier's body waited. Emma looked at the blond-haired handsome man and a tear slid down her cheek. She stared at his chest, willing him to start breathing again. After a moment she stopped fooling herself. Together Emma and Jennie prepared the body for burial and then with their mother's help, and that of some neighbors, they buried the soldier beside her father in the family plot. Today would be a day Emma would never forget.

Just the Facts

Emma Sansom was born June 2, 1847 at Social Circle, Walton County, Georgia. Her father was Micajah Sansom, Jr. He married Lamila (also known as Permelia and Lemilia) Barfield Vann in Jasper County, Georgia.

When Emma was 5 years old, in 1852, her family moved to a one-story farmhouse, consisting of a hallway with two or three rooms on each side, along Black Creek, near Gadsden, Alabama. Her father died there in 1859.

Emma is described as small, slender, with dark auburn hair, dark blue eyes, large smiling mouth, and even white teeth. In a 1963 paper written by Sarah Kathleen Brown, called "Emma Sansom: Civil War Heroine" Emma is described as popular with everyone who knew her, because of her gentle, cheerful and laughing way, though she could also be serious when needed.

Emma had several siblings. Her brothers were Orren, William, John, Joe, Rufus, and Tom. Her sisters were Liza, Mary, Anne, Martha, and Jennie. In 1855, the oldest three boys moved to Texas where they lived the rest of their lives. In 1861, Rufus joined the 19th Alabama Infantry.

Ironically, he was captured by the Yankees the very morning that Emma helped General Forrest.

The incident on May 2, 1863, occurred as General Nathan Bedford Forrest was chasing Colonel Abel Streight across Alabama. Forrest fought Streight for days before arriving at the Sansom's little farm on Black Creek.

Most of the dialogue used in the story was accurate. The facts, of course, are true. Emma rode behind General Forrest and showed him where to cross the river. She also received a note from him written with lead pencil on a stained piece of account paper, which proved to the doubtful Yankees that the incident happened. The note read something like this (though there are conflicting versions in various sources):

> *Hed Quaters In Sadle*
> *May 2, 1863*
> *My highest Regardes to Miss Ema Sanson for hir gallant conduct while my forse was skirmishing with the Federals a cross Black Creek near Gadesden Allabama*
>
> *N. B. Forrest*
> *Brig Genl*
> *Comding N. Ala–*

Did you notice General Forrest wrote that his headquarters was in his saddle? That was because he had been chasing Streight for days, and hadn't had chance to set up a real headquarters. Emma gave the original note to Dr. John Allen Wyeth many years later. Dr. Wyeth wrote a biography of Forrest in 1901, which he dedicated to Emma.

The Confederate Congress voted to give her a gold medal and the Alabama legislature voted to give her a section of land which she never received. In 1899 the Alabama state legislature voted to give her 640 acres of land to express their "admiration and gratitude."

Emma married Christopher Bullard Johnson in 1864. Christopher served in the 10th Alabama Regiment, C.S.A. during the Civil War. They moved to Calloway, Texas, in 1879. They had eight children. The first child was named Mattie Forrest Johnson, but she died while still an infant. She is buried next to Emma's father in the family burial plot at Black Creek. Emma's husband died in 1887.

Emma died August 22, 1900 in Calloway, Texas, and is buried in Little Mound Baptist Church Cemetery there, along with her mother and her sister Martha Sansom McKinney.

Emma's Ballad

A Ballad of Emma Sansom

The courage of man is one thing, but that of a maid is more,
For blood is blood, and death is death, and grim is the battle gore,
And the rose that blooms, tho' blistered by the sleet of an open sky,
Is fairer than its sisters are
Who sleep in the hothouse nigh.

Word came up to Forrest that Streight was on a raid—
Two thousand booted bayonets were riding down the glade,
Eight thousand were before him—he was holding Dodge at bay,
But he turned on his heels like the twist of a steel,
And was off at the break of day.

A fight to the death in the valley, and a fight to the death on the hill
But still Streight thunder'd southward, and Forrest followed still.
And the goaded hollows bellow'd to the bay of the rebel gun—
For Forrest was hot as a solid shot
When its fight is just begun.

*   *   *

A midnight fight on the mountain, and a daybreak fight in the glen,
And when Streight stopped for water he had lost three hundred men.
But he gained the bridge at the river and planted his batteries there,
And the halt of the gray was a hound at bay,
And the blue—a wolf in his lair.

And out from the bridge at the river a white heat lightning came,
Like the hungry tongues of a forest fire, with the autumn woods aflame;
And the death-smoke burst above them, and the death-heat blazed below,
But the men in gray cheered the smoke away,
And bared their breast to the blow.

"To the ford!, To the ford!" rang the bugle—"and flank the enemy out!"
And quick to the right the gray lines wheel and answer with a shout.
But the river was mad and swollen—to left—to right—no ford—
And still the sting of the maddened thing
At the bridge, and still the goad.

Then out from a nearby cabin a mountain maiden came,
Her cheeks were banks of snowdrifts, but her eyes were skies of flame,
And she drew her sunbonnet closer as the bullets whispered low—
(Lovers of lead) and one of them said:
"I'll clip a curl as I go!"

Straight through the blistering bullets she fled like a hunted doe,
While the hound-guns down at the river bayed in her wake below.
And around, their hot breath shifted, and behind, their pattering feet,
But still she fled through the thunder red,
And still through the lightning sleet.

And she stood at the General's stirrup, flushed as a mountain rose,
When the sun looks down in the morning, and the gray mist upward goes.
She stood at the General's stirrup and this was all she said:
"I'll lead the way to the ford today—
I'm a girl; but I'm not afraid!"

How the gray troops thronged around her! And then the rebel yell—
With that brave girl to lead them they would storm the gates of hell!
And they toss her behind the General, and again the echoes woke,
For she clung to him there with her floating hair
As the wild vine clings to the oak.

Down through the bullets she lead them, down through an unused road,
And, when the General dismounted to use his glass on the ford,
She spread her skirts before him (the troopers gave a cheer):
"Better get behind me, General,
For the bullets will hit you here!"
And then the balls came singing and ringing quick and hot,
But the gray troops gave them ball for ball and answer shot for shot.
"They have riddled your skirt," the General said, "I must take you out of this din."
"Oh, that's all right," she answered light—
"They are wounding my crinoline!"

And then, in a blaze of beauty, her sunbonnet off she took,
Right in the front she waved it high and at their lines it shook.
And the gallant bluecoats cheered her—ceased firing to a man,
And the graycoats rode through the bloody ford,
And again the race began.

John Trotwood Moore
(Tennessee)

From *The Blue and the Gray: The Best Poems of the Civil War,* compiled and edited by Claudius Meade Capps, ©1943 by Bruce Humphries, Inc., reprinted 1969 by arrangement, Library of Congress Catalog Card #70-75710, Granger Index Reprint Series, Books for Libraries Press, Freeport;182-5.

Emma Sansom Monument, Gadsden, Alabama. Photo by Betty Bolté.

Check It Out!

Cooper, Richard. *Emma Sansom: Ride to Glory!* Raleigh: Creative Productions, 1987

Henry, Robert Selph. *First with the Most: Forrest.* 150-1. New York: Smithmark Publishers Inc., 1991 by William S. Konecky Associates, Inc.

Hurst, Jack. *Nathan Bedford Forrest: A Biography.* 120-4. New York: Alfred A. Knopf, Inc., 1993.

Wills, Brian Steel. *A Battle from the Start: The Life of Nathan Bedford Forrest.* 115-6. New York: HarperCollins, 1992.

Wyeth, John Allan. *That Devil Forrest: The Life of General Nathan Bedford Forrest.* New York: Harper & Brothers, 1959. 186-190. Reprint, Baton Rouge: HarperCollins Publishers, Inc., 1989. [Dedicated to Emma Sansom, "A woman worthy of being remembered..."]

Online Resources

Emma's heroics are mentioned at Literary Alabama, *www.lib.ua.edu/literary/ctgads.htm.*

Emma Sansom High School has its own web page: *www.gcs.k12.al.us/emma_sansom.*

America's Civil War magazine printed an article about Emma in September 1996 and posted it online. Go to *www.thehistorynet.com/AmericasCivilWar/previous/0996.htm.*

Wait 'Til You See This!

The Gadsden Chapter of the United Daughters of the Confederacy erected a monument dedicated to Emma in 1906. At the time it was dedicated it was one of the few statues honoring American women in the country. The monument is located in Gadsden, Alabama, at the intersection of First and Broad Streets, near the bridge that crosses the river. The statue at the top is of Emma pointing the way, with a bas-relief sculpture on the side showing her riding behind General Forrest. In part, the inscription reads, "In memory of the Gadsden Alabama girl heroine, Emma Sansom,...A grateful people took the girl into their love and admiration, nor will this marble outlast the love and pride that her deed inspired."

The Alabama United Daughters of the Confederacy gave a life-size portrait of Emma to the State Department of Archives and History at Montgomery, Alabama.

Emma Sansom High School is located at 2210 West Meighan Boulevard, Gadsden, Alabama.

Near the school is the Emma Sansom Housing Development, which consists of a large number of apartment buildings.

On the bluff above the Coosa River in Gadsden is Emma Sansom Park.

Other Sources

Roach, Lt. A. C. *Prisoner of War and How Treated, Containing a History of Colonel Streight's Expedition to the Rear of Bragg's Army in the Spring of 1863, etc.* 32. Indianapolis: Railroad City Publishing House, 1865.

Sherr, Lynn and Jurate Kazickas. *Susan B. Anthony Slept Here: A Guide to American Women's Landmarks.* 2-3. New York: Random House, 1994.

Wiley, Bell Irvin. *Confederate Women.* 143. Westport: Greenwood Press, 1975.

WINNIE MAE MURPHREE

1863

Southern Hospitality

Winnie Mae finished clearing the dishes from the oak table, while her older sister Celia swept the floor of the small home. Song birds entertained the girls through the open window. Supper had been a quiet meal for the two sisters, waiting tensely to hear when their brother's child was born. Winnie Mae longed to see her new niece or nephew, but she had chores to finish.

"Listen," Winnie Mae said, pausing. "I hear a wagon coming." A thrill of fear rippled along her spine. Were their visitors friend or foe?

"Maybe Ma and Aaron are back," Celia replied, hurrying to the window.

Winnie Mae peeked over Celia's shoulder. A small wagon turned into the clearing with her younger brother driving. She rushed out the door, leaving it standing open behind her. She ran down the front steps and across the yard to meet her mother.

"How is Arminda?" Winnie Mae asked breathlessly. "Did she have the baby? Was it a boy or a girl?"

"Slow down, child." Winnie Mae's mother, Sarah Easley Murphree, stepped down from the wagon and took her daughter's hand. A smile burst onto her face. "It's a little girl."

"A niece!" Winnie Mae cried. "What's her name?"

"Mary Matilda Murphree. And just wait until Isaac sees how sweet she is," Sarah said. Winnie Mae noticed a shadow of worry cross her mother's face, understanding she was concerned her son wouldn't return from fighting with the Confederate army. He just had to come home to see his daughter though, Winnie Mae vowed.

"Did Arminda have a hard time, Ma?" Celia asked from the shade of the porch. "Did your jug of spirits help her?"

"She did fine," Sarah said, walking briskly up the steps and into the house. "I didn't use much of the liquor at all."

Winnie Mae's mother told them the events of the morning while she ate her supper. "After bit, Aaron will take you two over there and you can see what needs to be done."

"That's fine, Ma," Celia said. At 21 years old Celia was a pretty woman, though she had a stern mouth when she wasn't smiling. Luckily, she smiled easily and her dark eyes twinkled when she was happy. "I'm sure she could use our help today of all days."

"Yes, and we can hold our niece," Winnie Mae added. Her 18 years' experience on a small farm had prepared her for helping in any manner of situation, and this one in particular seemed to be more fun than work. She smiled at the thought of holding the tiny baby. Would the baby look more like Isaac or Arminda? Would she have the Murphree mouth? Would the baby's eyes be dark like Celia's, or lighter like her own?

Winnie Mae Murphree. Photo from The Heritage of Blount County.

Early that afternoon, Aaron drove them the half-mile to Arminda's house. The buckboard was pulled by two mares, each with a mule colt tagging along. Winnie Mae's brother was proud of the horses and colts. Even though only 15, he had high hopes for them. Aaron halted the wagon at the hitching post and securely tied the mares. Horses were too valuable during the Civil War to take any chances.

Winnie Mae was the first one inside the small, yet comfortable, home.

"Arminda! Congratulations!" Winnie Mae cried as she hurried to her sister-in-law's side and gave her a gentle hug. "Where's little Mary?"

"In her bassinet, napping," Arminda replied, quietly.

Winnie Mae took the hint and lowered her own voice. "I'm so happy for you," she whispered. Peeking into the bassinet, she saw the dark hair and closed eyes of her new niece. Glancing up, she smiled at Arminda. "You're so lucky."

"Your turn will come soon enough, Winnie Mae," Arminda replied. "You don't need to rush things. You can come here any time and play with Mary."

"I'd love that," Winnie Mae said, memorizing each detail of the slumbering face.

Light footsteps on the floor announced Celia's arrival. "Congratulations, Arminda," she said with a merry smile. "So we have a new member of the Murphree clan, don't we?"

"Yes. I only wish Isaac were here," Arminda replied. Her smile broke as tears threatened to fall.

"I know you must," Celia said, hugging Arminda.

"You have us to help, though," Winnie Mae offered. "What can we do?"

"How sweet of you," Arminda said. "Let me think…."

Hoofbeats outside interrupted the ladies.

"Who could that be?" Arminda asked.

Winnie Mae hurried to the window. "Union soldiers! Three of them."

"Come away from the window, Winnie Mae," Celia said tensely.

"They've killed Aaron's colts!"

"Winnie Mae, come away, now," Celia urged.

Arminda gathered her sleeping baby and, with a strained look, slipped into a back room, closing the door behind her. Celia and Winnie Mae exchanged glances and then hurried into the kitchen. As Celia closed the door leading to the rest of the house, a soldier burst through the outer door.

"May we help you?" Celia asked.

"You sure can, hon. Just stand there while I look around some," the soldier said. He searched the cabinets and drawers for guns and medical supplies. Winnie opened her mouth to object, but Celia frowned her into silence.

The soldier spotted the jug of spirits, used earlier to relieve the pains of childbirth, resting on the table. "What's this?" he asked. He pulled the stopper out and sniffed. "Seeing as we're here in the South, you can just make me and my buddies some of them mint juleps you all are so famous for."

"Mint juleps?" Celia asked, astounded.

"Yep, and right now." The soldier angled his gun in Celia and Winnie Mae's direction.

"If you insist," Celia said. Turning to Winnie Mae she said, "I'll get the mint from the well-curbing, if you'll get some fresh honey."

Silently, Winnie Mae walked past the soldier, Celia behind her. Once outside, they saw Aaron standing over the two dead mule colts. Another soldier had the two mares unhitched from the buckboard and waiting at one side of the clearing for his fellow soldiers to be ready to return to their camp. Celia gasped at the horrific sight, then strode briskly to the well and snatched several sprigs of mint from their stalks. Winnie Mae caught Aaron's eye and nodded at him, letting him know she shared his loss, then she walked quickly to the barn, thinking hard all the way. Surely these thugs could be stopped.

She found a fresh crock of honey and returned to the house, praying for inspiration with every step. Once inside, her gaze fell upon a small vial of toothache medicine sitting by the sink. Before anyone noticed her intent, she grabbed the vial and poured its contents into the crock of honey.

Celia Murphree. Photo from The Heritage of Blount County.

"Winnie, where's that honey?" Celia asked, her voice a note higher than normal.

Suppressing a smile, she handed the crock to her sister.

Seeing the pitchers of mint juleps ready, the soldier grinned and opened the door. Celia led the way onto the porch with the pitcher, Winnie Mae following with three glasses. The men sat down in the chairs on the porch and eagerly accepted the refreshing drinks. Aaron watched sullenly and silently beside his dead colts. Winnie Mae could see tears on his face.

"Woman, another round!"

Celia flinched, but obliged. Winnie Mae hoped the sedative would have an effect soon.

As the men sloshed the drinks into their mouths, dribbling some down their faces in the process, Winnie Mae saw their eyelids start to close. Come on, fall asleep already, she thought. She dared a glance at Celia, who watched with surprise as the men fell out of their chairs and onto the ground.

"What happened?" Celia asked, perplexed.

"Toothache powder," Winnie Mae said, laughing.

"What do we do with these vermin now?" Aaron asked.

Suddenly, a gun battle erupted from beyond the clearing. Silence fell. The gunfire had sounded from Royal Crossing, a junction of the Black Warrior River, not far from the house.

"I guess that's my answer," Aaron said. "Wait here."

Aaron sprinted for the woods and disappeared into them. Winnie Mae prayed he'd return safely. She looked at her sister, and saw her staring intently at the trees. Movement in the branches caused Winnie Mae to look back, just in time to see Aaron come running across the clearing.

"It's the Confederates, and cousin Mace is with them!"

"Thank God he's alive," Celia said. "What are we going to do with these men?"

"Get their guns, and turn them over to the Confederates," Winnie Mae said.

The three pulled the guns away from the sleeping men. Celia and Winnie Mae each picked up a gun, checked that it was loaded, and aimed it at the men.

"Aaron, douse them with water," Celia requested.

"I'd rather hit them with a pole-axe like they did to my mule colts," Aaron said, anger and grief mixed in his voice.

"I know, but please wake them with water," Celia said. "You don't really want to harm them, even as angry as you feel right now."

Winnie Mae didn't think Aaron agreed with Celia, but he went along with her plan. He grabbed the water bucket from the well and threw the water on the three men. They awoke, spluttering and bleary-eyed.

"Hold still!" Celia commanded.

Shock instantly replaced the sleepiness on the soldiers' faces. Warily they stood and faced their captors.

"All right, march!" Celia said, motioning toward the clearing.

Winnie Mae fell in beside Celia and they herded the men across the clearing and down the road to the Confederate camp.

When they walked into camp, Confederate soldiers surrounded the three Union soldiers, while the girls were taken to General Forrest to explain what had happened.

Winnie Mae and Celia each rode proudly out of camp on a new handsome mare, freshly captured from Colonel Abel D. Streight, as a gift from General Nathan B. Forrest for their bravery.

A new niece, three captured soldiers, and two new mares. What a day, Winnie Mae thought with a smile. She couldn't wait to tell Ma.

Just the Facts

(Author's Note: Not much written material can be found on the Murphrees, so some details in the above story may not be accurate.)

Winnie Mae Murphree was born May 12, 1844, probably in Blount County, Alabama. Her sister Celia was born in 1841. Her father was Elijah Murphree and her mother was Sarah Easley Murphree. Winnie Mae's father operated a corn and wheat mill, a blacksmith shop, cotton gin, and also farmed two hundred acres of land. The property was located in Blount County along the Little Warrior River, about four miles east of Royal.

Winnie Mae had at least six brothers: William, Bailey, Ben, Levi, Isaac, and Aaron. Three of them—Ben, Levi, and Isaac—were killed during the Civil War.

Winnie Mae's brother, Isaac, married Arminda Reid, and they had a baby girl named Mary Matilda Murphree on May 1, 1863. Winnie Mae's mother helped with the birthing, then sent Winnie Mae and Celia over in the afternoon to help out. Brother Aaron, who was 15 years old, drove the buckboard.

About the same time, Colonel Streight's Division of the Union Army was crossing the Black Warrior River at Royal Crossing. Colonel Streight needed fresh horses and sent several calvarymen to confiscate some. The three soldiers saw Aaron's mares and colts. One soldier confiscated the mares, killing the colts so they couldn't grow up and be used by the Rebels. Another looked for more horses in the barn, and a third went into the house looking for guns and medical supplies. This third man is the one reported to have asked for mint juleps.

An historical marker now stands near where the Murphree sisters turned over the soldiers to General Forrest. Photo by Betty Bolté.

Winnie Mae supposedly put a morphine-type medicine into the honey and gave it to Celia, who knew nothing about the addition. After two rounds, the men passed out on the ground. Celia and Winnie Mae took their guns and asked Aaron to douse them with water. His reply was that he "preferred to douse their heads with a pole-axe as they had done to his mule colts." Celia prevailed and he used water instead. Then Celia and Winnie Mae marched the three men into the Confederate bivouac located at Royal Crossing. General Forrest gave each of the girls a handsome mare as a reward for their bravery.

Celia married John C. Reneau in the spring of 1864. They had two sons and four daughters: Albert H., Retty A., Sarah Louisa, Arta C., Delia, and Myrtle. Those six children gave Celia and John seventy grandchildren. Celia died in 1899, and John in 1910.

Winnie married Asa Bynum in Blount County, Alabama in 1865, and they moved to Ellis County, Texas. Asa had been an excellent soldier in the Confederate Army. His parents were James and Katie Praytor Bynum. He was also the grandson of American Revolutionary War veterans Isaac Bynum and Solomon Murphree.

Winnie and Asa had a number of children, though sources vary on how many. Some sources say Winnie and Asa only had five children, others say ten. Albert was born May 15, 1879 and died December 3, 1899. Maud was born March 10, 1883 and died November 13 (18), 1899. Murty (Myrtle; Myrtie) A. was born November 22, 1886 and died October (November) 7, 1887. Other children are listed as son Asberry and daughters Adaline, Modelia, Sarah, Ida, Celia, and Mary. Celia, Albert, Mary, Maude, and Murty were all born in Ellis County, Texas; no place of birth is listed for the remaining children.

Winnie's headstone says "Winnie S. Bynum." Photo by Betty Bolté.

Winnie died from unknown causes on November 29, 1899, the same year as Celia. (Notice that she also died between her children Maud and Albert, in the space of a few weeks.) She is buried in the Oak Branch Cemetery, south of Dallas, Texas, along with some of her children, and later her husband. Asa died July 18, 1907, more than seven years after his family was buried.

Winnie's brother Aaron married Sarah Kathryn Cornelius about 1870. They moved to Lancaster, in Ellis County, Texas. They had ten children. Aaron died in 1914 and is buried somewhere near Lancaster.

Check It Out!

You won't find any books on the Murphree sisters. However, you can request a copy of their story (in The Heritage of Blount County, 1989) from the Department of Archives and History, located in Montgomery, Alabama. (Ref.–County Blount, 976.172, H548, 1989; #ALAV93-B94)

Wait 'Til You See This!

An historical marker stands among bushes along Alabama Highway 26 at Royal, near Blountsville, Alabama. The marker reads:

> *EXPLOIT OF MURPHREE SISTERS–Incident of May 1, 1863 during Streight (Union flag)–Forrest (Confederate flag) Campaign. Three prowling Union soldiers invaded home of sister-in-law of Celia and Winnie Mae Murphree taking food, drink; killing two colts. When soldiers fell asleep, these two young girls took rifles, marched soldiers to headquarters of General Forrest, bivouacked at Royal Crossing on Warrior River.*

Winnie is buried in the Oak Branch Cemetery in Ellis County, Texas. The cemetery is south of Dallas. To get there, from I-35, turn west onto F.M. 66 and follow to Oak Branch Road. Turn north and go 1.5 miles to the cemetery on the right side of the road. Or you can exit I-35 at F.M. 1446 and follow it west to Oak Branch, turn south and drive about 2 miles to the cemetery on your left. The five graves, of Winnie, Asa, and their three children, are located near the center of the cemetery.

Winnie's headstone reads:

Winnie S. Bynum
Wife of Asa Bynum
Born May 12, 1844
Died Nov 29, 1899

We miss thee from our home dear mother
We miss thee from thy place,
A shadow o'er our life is cast,
We miss the sunshine of thy face.

Celia and John Reneau are buried at Antioch Cemetery on Straight Mountain in Blount County, Alabama. Their markers read:
Celia Reneau
1841-1899

John C. Reneau
1836-1910

Other Sources

Sherr, Lynn and Jurate Kazickas. *Susan B. Anthony Slept Here: A Guide to American Women's Landmarks.* 2. New York: Random House, 1994.

LAVINIA ELLEN REAM

1864

Sculpting the Man of Sorrow

Vinnie walked along the streets of Washington, D.C., admiring the many statues and art work displayed among the trees and buildings. Her job at the Postal Service left her feeling cramped and dirty. Now she could study the city's many fine examples of sculpture and painting.

The April sunshine shone on a city that struggled against looking more like an army camp than a town. The Civil War had begun, and now the dirt streets became very muddy as the spring rains fell and the snow melted. Between the formal buildings stood tents. People sold food and goods from wagons along the street. The Washington Monument was only partially completed, its outline against the sky showing where work had stopped on it in order for the men to fight in the war. Likewise, the Capitol dome was not finished, beams poking through the open roof. Despite the war, President Abraham Lincoln ordered that work continue on the dome as a sign of solidarity.

Vinnie at 15 years old, with her bust of Lincoln. Courtesy Library of Congress.

Vinnie briefly held a perfumed handkerchief to her nose, to mask the awful smell of the sewage running along the canal. She missed the open air and lakes of Wisconsin, her home state. Now at just 16 years old, her family had moved to Washington so her father could join a Capitol guard detail to protect the president during the war.

She remembered that her mother was waiting for her at their home on B Street North. "I've got to get home," she said aloud to herself. There were epaulets (fringed shoulder pads) to sew for the various uniformed men in town to wear on their uniform shoulders. The little money they made from sewing meant a lot to the Ream family as they struggled to make ends meet.

As she hurried up Pennsylvania Street, she noticed President Lincoln riding down the street. His guards rode behind him, trying to keep up with the determined man. She saw a sadness etched into his face, leaving lines around his mouth and eyes. His stovepipe hat and old shawl were pulled around him as he hurried by, on some government business, no doubt.

Vinnie strode down the muddy street, the picture of Lincoln's sadness in her mind.

Before she started working at the Post Office in 1862, she spent most days studying at home. She liked reading poetry by Edgar Allan Poe and Lord Byron, and sometimes tried her own hand at writing poetry. She was always surprised and happy when a newspaper would print one of her poems. She loved to sing, and often sang for the soldiers in concert. She was even paid $150 a year to sing at the E Street Baptist Church. She didn't bother with the simple pleasures her friends enjoyed, feeling that she was supposed to do something important with her life. She wanted to be ready for whatever that special work might be.

One day in 1863, Vinnie had been walking along Pennsylvania Avenue as she loved to do. Suddenly a man with a beard and bright eyes appeared before her. She smiled at him, recognizing an old family friend.

"You must be little Vinnie Ream," he said. He noticed her long, brown curls and dark eyes. She had grown into a beautiful girl.

"Yes, and you must be Major Rollins."

Major James S. Rollins had been a friend since Vinnie had attended the Christian College, in Columbia, Missouri, in 1857. He had been a land lawyer then, and played a big part in starting the University of Missouri in 1841. He had noticed how easily Vinnie learned. Now, Major Rollins had been elected to the Congress to represent Boone County, Missouri.

"I've been looking for you, Vinnie," Major Rollins said. "Christian College is trying to find a photograph of you to put in the school library."

"Of me?" Vinnie asked. She was delighted and surprised. She remembered her many friends from school. She had studied piano and vocal music, and enjoyed writing songs. She had even written a school song they sang while she was there. She wondered if they still sang it. In 1858, when she was 11, her poem called "Heart Longings" was published. She'd been sad to leave her friends behind when her father moved the family to Little Rock, Arkansas, in late 1859.

"Yes, your sketch of Martha Washington still hangs in the library. Now they want a photograph of you. They asked me to see if you would agree."

"We'll have to ask Mother," Vinnie said.

When the two arrived home, Major Rollins asked Mrs. Ream if he could have a photograph made of Vinnie. (In those days, only professional photographers owned a camera and knew how to make pictures.) Receiving her permission, he arranged to return the next day and escort her to the photographer's studio. When he arrived, he told Vinnie he had changed his mind about the photograph.

"I think it would be better to have a sculpture made instead. I know a man, the finest sculptor in America, whose studio is in the lower level of the Capitol. His name is Clark Mills. I'm sure he would agree to create a sculpture of you."

So the pair headed for the studio. Vinnie couldn't believe she would actually meet Clark Mills. She had heard of him before, mainly because she had studied art and sculpture for many years. She had taken an interest in working with clay as a young girl. In 1851, when she was four, her family had moved for awhile to Washington, D.C. Then, she had visited the Pennsylvania Avenue studio of Benjamin Paul Akers, where he let her sing songs while she shaped the wet clay. Later, while attending the Christian College in Missouri, Major Rollins had suggested that she study art. She told him that she wanted to do sculpture, and he had encouraged her. Now he was taking her to meet a real sculptor.

Vinnie's portrait takes center stage in this exhibit of her life at the Eastern Trails Museum in Vinita, Oklahoma. Photo by Chris Bolté.

When they entered the makeshift studio, Vinnie saw an older man, about 50 years old. The studio held an odd collection of objects. She saw a few marble busts, some fever and ague medicines, sketches, a hat filled with eggs, and a mix of machines.

After Major Rollins introduced Vinnie to Clark Mills, the sculptor set to work making a model of her features in clay. Vinnie watched, fascinated, yet a bit critically. Finally, she couldn't hold her tongue any longer.

"I can do that," she said.

"Why you vain little thing, you cannot." Mills kept working as he dismissed her claim.

"I would show you," Vinnie said, facing the challenge, "if I could get my hands on some of that clay."

A touch upset, Mills tossed a lump of clay to Vinnie then turned back to his own work. Vinnie, meanwhile, pushed and pulled and shaped the clay into an Indian chief's head, including the feather headdress. Vinnie's reward was a nod from Clark Mills, telling her she'd done a good job. Major Rollins, meanwhile, was so impressed by his little friend's ability that he kept a copy of the statue to put on his desk in his congressional office.

Vinnie worked with Clark for a while, learning about shaping the clay into the form she wanted it to be. The studio was a place that tired politicians visited to relax and talk. Before too long, Vinnie began creating bas-relief profile medallions of politicians such as James Nesmith, Richard Yates, and John Sherman. She also created a self-portrait bust she called "The Violet" because it had violets surrounding the lower edges of the bust to hide where the arms ended. As Vinnie's work became better, she got the idea of creating a bust of Abraham Lincoln from actual sittings. She asked some of the politicians if they would ask Lincoln, but most didn't want to bother the weary president. Finally, a few of her friends, including James Nesmith, asked Lincoln if he would sit for the young girl from Madison.

Lincoln had modeled for many artists and photographers, and refused the request. As they were about to leave, James Nesmith told Lincoln that Vinnie was nothing but a poor girl from the West, who had an artistic promise they wanted to help along. As he finished speaking, Lincoln considered the idea.

"Poor, is she?" he said. "Well, that's nothing agin' her."

Vinnie spent some time observing the president. She grew to know all his moods, and especially remembered his sadness over the death of his son, Willie. As she watched him, she tried to capture his sorrow in the sculpted bust.

When she was in his office, Lincoln would often sit slouched in his chair at the desk, his large feet out in front of him, his head nearly touching his chest, thinking. Sometimes, he would stand at the window and stare at the lawn outside, apparently imagining his little Willie playing, for he had tears on his face.

Vinnie's statue of Lincoln still stands in the Capitol Rotunda in Washington, D.C. Photo by Chris Bolté.

On Good Friday, April 14, 1865, Vinnie didn't go to the White House. She was nearly finished with the bust, so she stayed at her studio. She just had a few final touches to make to it, and she would be done.

"Vinnie, you're doing a fine job," Lincoln had told her. She smiled to herself as she worked. He had said it often.

Her parents went out for a walk after dinner that evening, and she worked at mounting pictures into a new album. Late that night, she heard a man yell as he ran past the house. Vinnie hurried to the window, and saw her parents standing on the steps.

"Lincoln has been shot! Lincoln has been shot!" the man cried as he continued down the street.

Lincoln had been watching the play *Our American Cousin* at Ford's Theatre, when John Wilkes Booth shot him in the back of the head. The president died the next day.

Lincoln's death devastated Vinnie. She spent days in bed, crying. During that time, she thought of little but Lincoln, until his image and his memory were burned into her mind. The following Tuesday, April 18, Vinnie and her parents were among the hundreds of mourners who filed past Abraham Lincoln's casket in the East Room of the Executive Mansion. Then on Friday, April 21, the casket was loaded onto a train, with the casket of little Willie at his feet, and they began the trip to Springfield, Illinois, to be buried.

Soon everyone on Capitol Hill was talking about creating a life-size statue of Lincoln and placing it in the Rotunda of the Capitol. Every sculptor who thought he could do the job began planning the statue.

Senator Ross, a friend of the family, suggested that Vinnie should also compete to create the statue.

"But I'm a woman," she said.

Her mother would have none of that attitude. She urged Vinnie to accept the senator's challenge, and submit a proposal for creating the statue. No one had considered that Vinnie would be interested in trying the project, especially because she was only 18 and had little experience. And of course, she was a woman. The press demanded, "Who is Vinnie Ream?"

Her friends wrote a petition in favor of Vinnie creating the statue and it was signed by many important people on Capitol Hill. They included her teacher Clark Mills, President Andrew Johnson, General Ulysses S. Grant, General George A. Custer, as well as many senators and House representatives. The Ream Commission, as it was called, was presented to the House on July 26, 1866. The vote was 57 yeas, 7 nays. Having passed in the House, the commission was sent to the Senate. The Senate debated the commission on July 27, 1866. After a lengthy exchange between Senator Charles Sumner of Massachusetts and the rest of the Senate, the final vote was 23 yeas, 9 nays. Vinnie—the youngest person and the only woman competing—was given the huge task of creating a marble statue of the late President Abraham Lincoln.

Immediately, there was an uproar in the local newspapers about this unknown artist being awarded such an important job at a cost of $10,000. Vinnie ignored the comments, knowing that they didn't know her and therefore their opinions didn't matter. She went about the business of creating the clay model from which the marble statue would be carved. First, an iron framework was put together to support the clay. Vinnie worked at creating Lincoln's image, knowing that she must put the true personality of the man into the lifeless mud. Many people doubted she could do it.

Vinnie wouldn't receive any money until the clay model was finished, then she would get a check for $5,000 upon the Congress' satisfaction. In order to afford to live and to create the model, she kept taking on commissions for other artwork.

At one point in the creation of the Lincoln statue, she decided that she wanted to use the suit of clothes he had worn when he was shot. He had worn a frock coat, vest, trousers, black silk cravat (tie), and a long cape with the lining embossed with an eagle biting two festoons (ribbons) on which were the words, "One Country, One Destiny." Mrs. Lincoln abruptly answered her letter requesting to borrow the suit:

> *Your letter has been received and I hasten to return an early reply. I shall be unable to comply with your request...As every friend my husband knew was familiar to me, and as your name was not on the list, consequently you could not have become familiar with the expression of his face, which was so variable, even to those and especially to myself, who had passed almost a lifetime studying its changes...Mary Todd Lincoln, Chicago, September 10, 1866.*

Vinnie realized that Mrs. Lincoln did not know that she had spent time with the president. And she knew that Mrs. Lincoln had been kept in the dark because she was known to be very jealous of her husband and of those who spent time with him, especially women. Vinnie kept trying to find a way to borrow the clothes. She learned that Mrs. Lincoln gave them to the bodyguard who had protected her husband. Through the help of some friends, Vinnie finally received permission to use the clothes and they arrived at her studio on April 22, 1867.

She picked up the coat, noticing the blood stains, and with trembling fingers began to take measurements. Vinnie forced back tears and focused on her work.

She kept her studio open so everyone could monitor the progress of the statue. She greeted her visitors with a firm handshake, bordering on manly. She wrote later:

> *In the bright and rambling discussions of men and things which took place in my studio were told many tales of the war —its privations, its hardships and sufferings —by the gallant soldiers who came to see how the statue was developing. Some came on crutches and told of how father and son, brother and brother had met upon the battlefield only to die in each others arms. Gettysburg was often mentioned and*

then like a sacred poem intoned upon the organ came the memory of
Lincoln's inspired words upon that blood-stained field....

Finally, after several years, she finished the clay model. Then she had a plaster cast of the model made by a New York company led by Henry Kirke Brown. On January 30, 1869, Vinnie officially told the Senate that the plaster model was completed. With the notice came a request for payment of $5,000.

Vinnie read in the newspaper a description of her model:

... The features of Mr. Lincoln are admirably rendered; and it was this faithful delineation of character which obtained for Miss Ream the Commission for this statue over many able competitors. The head and features are forcibly, yet truthfully, modeled; the hair boldly managed in flowing masses as by the skill of experience; and the expression of sadness mingled with benevolence is touchingly portrayed, well conceived and appropriate to the expression and meaning of the statue.

"The head bending slightly forward and downward seems to regard with anxious solicitude the multitude of a newly-liberated people to whom is presented by the right hand the 'proclamation' of their emancipation. A long circular cloak covers the right shoulder and arm, falls backward off the left, being held partially under the forearm and caught up by the left hand, which grasps its ample folds as if in readiness to cover with the protecting mantle of the Government the defenseless beings who are to receive the inestimable boon of freedom. A beautiful thought of the artist aptly and ingeniously symbolized...

"The cloak is happily arranged to give breadth, as well as dignity to a very tall and meager figure; it plays also a useful part in aiding to support, where it touches the ground, the weight of the statue.

After another try at keeping the payment from her by Sumner and Howard based on prejudices of the day, Congress approved the amount on April 29, 1869. She received the payment in July.

Vinnie and her parents left for New York City on June 8, 1869, on their way to Rome to have the statue carved from marble. They sailed to Queenstown, England aboard the *Dana*. During the voyage, Vinnie entertained by singing songs and playing her guitar.

They spent several months in Europe, traveling and meeting new friends. Vinnie continued to create new statues in temporary studios she set up in various cities. She wrote:

> *The model for the Lincoln statue, the bust of Gustave Dore, and the likeness of Father Hyacinthe, seem to attract a great deal of attention. I have also in my studio a bust of Mrs. Fremont which I made in Paris, and a likeness of the great German painter Kaulbach, which I modeled in his studio in Munich.*

By December 15, she had begun studying French and had made the first corrections to the Lincoln statue. On January 7, 1870, a friend invited Vinnie to hear composer Franz Liszt play. His music moved her to tears, and they became great friends.

During all this, Vinnie received many letters and visits from men interested in courting her. She was flattered, but forced herself to keep her attention on her sculpting. The statue must come first.

On March 10, 1870, Vinnie signed with a Carrara, Italy sculptor, Thommaso Gagliardi, to rough out her Lincoln statue. They spent a great deal of time selecting the piece of marble to use, finally finding a piece of white marble without any flaws. She paid him one thousand American dollars to do the work and ship the statue to the Italian port of Leghorn.

The statue was ready for inspection by October of 1870. She made some last corrections to the work, and had it crated and sent to America.

Vinnie and her parents left for America on the *Abyssinia* at the end of October. The statue was unveiled for the public on January 25, 1871.

Vinnie heard clapping sweep across the room as the figure was uncovered. It continued for a long time. Vinnie looked at the gleaming marble and remembered the sad man with whom she'd spent so many days. All the hard work had been worth this moment.

Just the Facts

A great deal has been written and preserved about Vinnie Ream. She created many pieces of art, poetry, song, and many, many friends during her lifetime.

Lavinia Ellen Ream, known as Vinnie, was born September 25, 1847 in Madison, Wisconsin.

Vinnie's father was Robert Lee Ream, who was born in 1809 in Centre County, Pennsylvania. He was raised in a German-speaking family. He married Lavinia McDonald in 1835 at Brookfield, Ohio. Robert Ream learned to speak English, but never lost his German accent.

Vinnie's brother, Robert Ream II, was born in Ohio about 1839. Her sister, Cynthia Ann Ream, known as Mary, was born in 1844 in Madison, Wisconsin. Mary was one of the first white girls to be born in the Wisconsin area.

Vinnie's earliest playmates were Winnebago Indian children, because there were few if any other white children to play with. The Winnebago taught Vinnie how to draw and paint.

Vinnie's childhood was spent moving around quite a bit. Her father was a surveyor, and so would travel to find work. They lived at various times in Madison, Wisconsin; Little Rock and Ft. Smith, Arkansas; St. Joseph, Missouri; Wyandotte and Leavenworth, Kansas; and Washington, D.C.

When they moved to D.C. just at the beginning of the Civil War, they settled in a cottage at 325 B Street North. Her father joined a Capitol guard unit. Her brother Bob had enlisted in Woodruff's artillery battery in Arkansas, then later joined the Confederate cavalry. To earn money to support the family, Vinnie, her mother, and her sister, all sewed epaulets for the officers' uniforms.

After studying sculpture with Clark Mills for awhile, she began making medallion reliefs of politicians. Then she had the idea of creating a bust of Lincoln. She was given permission by Lincoln only because she was poor, like he had been when he was younger.

I came for half an hour every day. I was the merest slip of a child, weighing less than ninety pounds; and the contrast between the raw-boned man and me was indeed great. I sat demurely in my corner and begged Mr. Lincoln not to allow me to disturb him.

She went to the White House frequently, watching him, trying to capture his personality in clay.

I think that history is particularly correct in writing Lincoln down as the man of sorrow. The one great, lasting, all-dominating impression that I have always carried of Lincoln has been that of unfathomable sorrow, and it was this that I tried to put into my statue.

The death of Lincoln caused his memory to be locked in hers forever.

The success of the statue that I subsequently made was attributed to its trueness to the actual Lincoln. My ability to produce it was unquestionably due to those half-hours in the quiet of the President's office, and to the searing in of the image by the great tragedy.

In April 1866, Vinnie's friends encouraged her to apply for the commission to create a life-size marble statue of Lincoln. They helped write and circulate a petition, which was signed by many of the most powerful men in Washington. Congress granted the commission to her on July 28, 1866, with the contract for the statue signed on August 30, 1866.

The Admiral Farragut statue in Farragut Square, Washington, D.C. Photo by Chris Bolté.

During the years it took to make the statue, Vinnie's studio became a gathering place for the politicians. A few unhappy politicians accused her of trying to influence the outcome of the vote on whether to impeach President Andrew Johnson, Lincoln's former vice president. When the impeachment effort failed, the House Managers kicked Vinnie out of her studio as a way of getting even. Through persistence and friends, she managed to reclaim her studio so that she could complete her work.

She completed the clay model about January 27, 1869 and then had a plaster cast made. She and her parents left for England aboard the *Dana* on June 8, 1869. She took the plaster cast of the model to Carrara, Italy on March 10, 1870 to have Thommaso Gagliardi create the marble statue. They returned to America aboard the *Abyssinia* the last week of October, 1870. The unveiling of the Lincoln in the Rotunda of the Capitol in Washington, D.C. occurred on Wednesday, January 25, 1871.

Congress commissioned Vinnie—again after much debate—to create a statue of Admiral David Glasgow Farragut. Congress signed the contract on January 28, 1875. Vinnie cast the statue from the bronze propellor of Farragut's flagship, the *Hartford*, in which he had achieved his best success. The statue, resting on a base made out of Maine granite, stands on Farragut Square, on K Street between Sixteenth and Seventeenth Streets in Washington, D.C. It faces south and stands 10 feet high, with Farragut holding a marine glass in his left hand, and resting his left foot atop a block and tackle. Vinnie was paid $20,000 to create the statue.

During the six years she spent making the Farragut, First Lieutenant Richard Hoxie proposed to her. She refused him, saying her work must come first. Only after Mrs. Farragut advised her to go ahead and marry, that the statue would wait, did Vinnie accept the proposal.

She married Lieutenant Richard Leveridge Hoxie on May 28, 1878. Lieutenant Hoxie was assigned to the Corps of Engineers, United States Army.

The unveiling and dedication of the Farragut occurred on April 25, 1881 amidst much ceremony. One (unidentified) local paper reported on the occasion:

> *It was an inspiring sight. Besides the vast multitude of civilians; the host of soldiers and sailors, in their glittering uniforms; the rainbow hues of the Spring appareling of thousands of women; the decorated houses surrounding the square, glinting with flags and filled with bright faces from basement to roof–all were framed in the delicate interlacing of the young leaved trees and mounted by the snowy tracery of the delicate clouds, that fluttered like feathers against the warm blue of the April sky. President Garfield's speech was happy, as his speeches always are.*

Throughout her life, people wrote poems and songs dedicated to Vinnie. She also wrote songs and poems, some of which were performed or published.

Vinnie died at 6:00 a.m. in her Washington home on November 20, 1914. She had been ill for eight weeks prior to her death. Her home, located at 1632 K Street NW, was a place of hospitality, and people from around the world would visit her.

Funeral services were held at St. John's Church, Lafayette Square, on the Monday following her death at 2:30 p.m.. She was laid out in her wedding dress for viewing in her home, then buried at Arlington National Cemetery, Arlington, Virginia.

The *La Follette's Magazine*, of Madison, Wisconsin, said of her after her death: "None who knew her can ever forget her. Nor shall we ever expect to meet another like her. For she was different and belongs to the immortal great."

Check It Out!

Fiction

Brenner, Barbara. *Saving the President: What If Lincoln Lived.* New York: J. Messner, 1987.

Sappéy, Maureen Stack. *Letters from Vinnie.* Asheville: Front Street Books, 1999.

Nonfiction

Campbell, O.B. *The Story of Vinnie Ream.* Vinita: Eastern Trails Historical Society, (not dated).

Hoxie, Richard L. *Vinnie Ream.* Uncatalogued collection of letters and photographs during the period 1865-1878, printed for private distribution by R. L. Hoxie and the Press of Gibson Bros., Washington, D.C., 1908.

Hubbard, Freeman H. *Vinnie Ream and Mr. Lincoln.* New York: Whittlesey House, 1949.

Sherwood, Glenn V. *A Labor of Love: The Life and Art of Vinnie.* Hygiene, CO: SunShine Press Publications, 1997.

Simmons, Dawn Langley. *Vinnie Ream: the Story of the Girl Who Sculptured Lincoln.* By Gordon Langley Hall. New York: Holt, Rinehart and Winston, 1963. (Juvenile literature)

Online Resources

A complete, balanced and well-researched site about Vinnie can be found at *www.vinnieream.com*. It contains many photos of her and her work, as well as the text of several speeches she made.

To see a photo of her monument at Arlington Cemetery go to *http://findagrave.com/pictures/reamvinnie.html.*

You can read a short biography of Vinnie at*http://www.plgrm.com/ history/women/R/.*

You can see a photo of her statue of Sequoyah by going to *http://clerk-web.house.gov/greathall/statuary/statues/oks.htm.*

The Library of Congress has several manuscripts related to Vinnie that you can look up at *http://lcweb.loc.gov/rr/mss/guide/arts.html.*

Wait 'Til You See This!

Brigadier General Richard Hoxie had a monument built in 1915 in Vinnie's honor. It stands in Arlington Cemetery, in Section 3, on Miles Drive. The statue is a bronze likeness of her marble Sappho statue. His sense of loss is felt in the inscription "Words that would praise thee are impotent" engraved in the bronze plaque in the base along with her bas-relief profile. A stone bench faces the monument, inviting visitors to linger, as Vinnie would have wanted.

Vinnie's monument in Arlington National Cemetery features a statue of Sappho. Photo by Betty Bolté.

The site of the log cabin in which Vinnie was born is marked by a plaque on a low wall near the intersection of King and Webster Streets, Madison, Wisconsin.

The Wisconsin Historical Museum has one of her sculptures, "Spirit of the Carnival," on display.

Vinnie's statue, "The West," is on display at the Wisconsin State Capitol building.

The Vinnie Ream Hoxie House, where she and her husband spent many summers, is located at 310 South Lucas Street, Iowa City, Iowa. The house was called "Vinita" after the town (Vinita, Oklahoma).

A small collection of memorabilia and photographs, on loan from the Oklahoma Historical Society, is on display at the Eastern Trails Museum, in Vinita, Oklahoma. It is located at 215 West Illinois Avenue. Vinita was named after Vinnie by her friend, Col. Elias C. Boudinot, a Cherokee.

At the Capitol in Washington, D.C. are several of her works. Among them, the bust of Lincoln, the life-size statue of Lincoln in the Rotunda, and a life-size statue of Sequoyah. Many more statues, ideals, medallions, and busts are scattered across the country in various museums and private collections.

The bronze statue of Admiral David G. Farragut stands on Farragut Square, K Street between Sixteenth and Seventeenth Streets, Washington, D.C.

The mansion that Richard Hoxie built for his wife stood at 1632 K Street NW, Washington, D.C., overlooking her statue of Admiral Farragut. The house was on the southeast corner of K and Seventeenth Streets.

Other Sources

Hall, Gordon Langley. "The Girl Who Sculptured Lincoln." *Woman's Day*. February 1966.

Kelly, Tom. "New Stature for Teen-age Sculptress of Lincoln." *The Washington Times*. March 19, 1990.

Sherr, Lynn and Jurate Kazickas. *Susan B. Anthony Slept Here: A Guide to American Women's Landmarks*. 85,94,151,371-2,457,458,493. New York: Random House, 1994.

"Society Present Lincoln Apparel to Ford's." *The Capitol Dome*. A newsletter published by the United States Capitol Historical Society. April 1968. Vol 3, No 2.

KATE SHELLEY

1881

Saving the Train

Kate Shelley hung the last of the clothes on the line. She paused a moment to soak in the view of the Honey Creek valley, a view she saw every day yet never tired of seeing. Two railroad bridges at either side of the valley glistened in the early evening sunlight, one spanning Honey Creek and one the Des Moines River. Gray clouds collecting overhead cast shadows on the green meadows flanking the winding Honey Creek. Trees guarded the shores of the rivers, their leafy heads swaying in the building wind. Ever-darker clouds gathered as Kate watched. A whopper of a storm was brewing.

"Kate!" her mother called. She stood in the doorway of the house that was perched on the side of a steep hill.

"Coming!" Kate replied. She started toward the house, favoring her side where she'd hurt herself a few days earlier when she fell from the wagon. The grape arbor snuggled against the hill, bravely growing its sweet fruit. She noted the oat crop was faring well this year as she hurried across the yard. The Shelley farm sprawled up the hillside, but little of the land was suitable for growing crops. Ever since her father died three years earlier, Kate had taken on the running of the farm. She was proud of her successes in raising grapes and cereal grains.

"Yes, mother?" Kate asked. She noticed her mother looked worried. Sisters Mayme and Maggie quickly strode toward the wash lines.

"There's a storm kicking up," the Widow Shelley said, coming down the steps and pointing to the darkening sky.

A blinding flash of lightning streaked across the sky, followed instantly by deafening thunder.

"Hurry, girls!" Widow Shelley called out.

Kate ran to help her sisters bring in the laundry, grabbing the skirts and blouses and "unmentionables" from the lines. She heard the whistle of a train that was out on the tracks, daring the storm. Most of the clothes were almost dry, though raindrops began splattering the ground as they ran across the yard and up the steps to the safety of the porch.

Pausing to survey the farm yard, Kate realized the sky had become dark as night, while lightning snaked and exploded across the clouds. Thunder continued to roll and crash above her head as the rain arrived in cascading sheets. Water washed across the porch, forcing Kate inside to keep dry.

"What an awful storm," Kate's youngest sister Mayme said, hugging herself tightly. Kate's other sister Margaret joined Mayme, wrapping a comforting arm across the younger girl's shoulders.

"We'll be fine," Widow Shelley said.

Kate at 15 years old. Courtesy Boone Historical Society.

The three women watched out the window at the flashes of light. As the Widow Shelley's oldest child, Kate was responsible for setting a good example for her younger siblings. She tried to not flinch when the thunder reverberated inside the house. Mayme began to cry as the storm worsened. With each flash, Kate could see that Honey Creek had swollen into a raging river and was gathering force and speed. Water ran down the hill behind the house, until the water actually poured into the house

Kate and her sisters jumped as a series of white flashes outside the window were followed immediately by a crash of thunder that shook the window panes.

"Let's sit at the table, away from the window," Kate's mother said.

Kate thought of the poor animals huddled inside the barn and decided she must check on their safety. Without the livestock, they would have little money or food this winter.

"I'm going to see to the animals," Kate said, heading for the door.

Kate's mother nodded and said, "Be careful out there."

Kate looked at her mother for a moment. "I'll be back."

Kate fought her way through the wind and rain to the stable. Water surrounded the barn. Kate sloshed through the flooded yard and hurried inside. She let the horses and cows out to fend for themselves, knowing they would seek higher ground quicker on their own. In one corner of the barn, on a mound of hay, Kate spied a few little pigs that she also put outside. The water was knee deep by the time she cleared out the barn and returned to the house.

The storm started at six o'clock in the evening and raged for hours. Kate, her mother, Mayme, and Maggie, watched the storm outside. As time went on, they began to worry about the trains trying to cross the railroad bridges over the raging streams and rivers.

"Is that an engine passing over the bridge?" Kate asked, horrified.

"Don't worry, Kate. No trains will be dispatched in this storm," Kate's mother said.

"I pray they don't." Kate clasped her hands in her lap, to stop them from trembling.

As the hour approached midnight, the storm subsided somewhat. Kate rested upon her bed, trying to force herself to forget the storm and go to sleep. Suddenly, she heard the rumble of a train as it crossed the long railroad bridge heading east. Kate listened intently, hoping they would make it across. Suddenly, the train's bell clanged twice, then the sound of timbers splitting was followed by the eerie hiss of steam.

"Oh, Mother!" Kate cried. She jumped from her bed and ran to the kitchen. Everyone gathered, concern on their faces. Kate spoke first. "It's No. 11! They've gone down Honey Creek Bridge!"

"Oh, no!" Maggie said. "Those poor men."

"What were they doing out in this anyway?" Mayme said, peering out the window at the storm.

"Checking the tracks, most likely," Widow Shelley said. "There's nothing we can do."

The silence that followed the crash of the engine into the swollen river filled the lull in the storm. The foursome huddled by the window. Kate wanted to do something, anything to help the men on that engine. There must be a way, she thought, to rescue them.

"There'll be a passenger train from the West along soon," Kate said, trying to remain calm. "I have to go help the men in the river, and try to stop that passenger train."

"Kate, you can't go out in this storm," Widow Shelley said. "What could you possibly do?"

The Kate Shelley High Bridge. Courtesy Boone Historical Society.

Kate heard her mother's and sisters' pleas, but they couldn't change her mind. She must go.

"Go then in the name of God, and do what you can," Kate's mother said. Tears danced in her eyes as she hugged her oldest daughter.

Kate put on an old skirt and jacket, then jammed a straw hat snugly onto her head.

"You'll need a lantern," her mother said.

"I don't have one," Kate replied. She looked around the cozy kitchen and spied the frame of an old lantern and a miners lamp. She hung the miners lamp inside the frame of the lantern, then filled the little lamp. She tore a strip of fabric from an old flannel skirt and used it as a wick. Pleased with her ingenuity, she lit the lamp. Now she was ready to brave the storm.

She opened the door and the fury of the storm washed over her, drowning out the crying of her mother and sisters behind her. She knew they were praying to God to keep her safe as she ventured outside.

The pretty little valley was filled with water, rushing through and over the railroad track. Kate chose a path that took her around the bluff and in a semi-circle behind her house. She made her way around the house and then turned east. The path she forged was difficult, pressing through bushes and brambles as she went. She reached and then followed the track to the broken bridge over Honey Creek. Her lantern helped her find where to step, but as she neared the bridge she couldn't see where the engine had fallen, nor where the men onboard might be. A white blaze of lightning illuminated the scene, and she saw the engineer, Ed Wood, clinging to a submerged tree. She saw that he was safe. Kate heard him call to her, but the din of the storm was so great she couldn't understand his words.

"I'll go get help!" she yelled back. She could tell from his puzzled expression that he hadn't heard her. "I'll be back!"

Kate turned and hurried towards the Moingona station on the other side of the high bridge to the west. The Des Moines River lay far below the high bridge. A gust of wind blew out Kate's lantern as she approached the trestle. Kate had been near this bridge before and knew how perilous crossing it on foot would be. Before her lay five hundred feet of track, with the railroad ties spaced more than a stride apart. To keep people from crossing the bridge on foot, the railroad company had added spikes to the ties. Kate took a deep breath, got down on her hands and knees and began the slow process of crossing the bridge. Her make-shift lantern hung useless from her hand as she placed each hand and knee.

After what seemed like years, Kate reached the center of the bridge. A flash of lightning spotlighted an immense tree careening toward the supports of the bridge. She held her breath, fearing the tree's impact would tear down the bridge from under her. Rain pelted her face as she watched the tree spin in the water, ever closer to where she clutched the rail. Terror forced her upright, her hands clasped in front of her, as she prayed to be saved. The tree spun once more and darted between the supports. Relief washed over her with the rain. More determined than ever, she continued her painful crossing.

Finally, she reached the ground on the other side of the raging river. She stood for a moment, catching her breath, thankful she'd made it. She could see the lights of the Moingona Station, almost a mile in the distance. Despite her injury from falling off the wagon, she ran to the station to spread the alarm about the fallen engine and the broken bridge.

Unfortunately, at first no one believed Kate's story. The people milling about the station, waiting for the storm to pass, looked at her in disbelief. The operator, Ike Fanzler, said, "The girl's lost her mind."

Kate's mouth fell open. Why wouldn't they believe her? A familiar face emerged from the sea of strangers. The agent of the Moingona Station, Mr. McIntyre, instantly recognized her despite her disheveled appearance and said, "My God! That's Kate Shelley." Kate knew Mr. McIntyre from the days when her father had been a section foreman for the railroad. She'd never before been so glad to see him.

A rescue party soon developed from the railroad personnel and townspeople. Pusher engine 230, waiting in the train yard, blasted its whistle, rousing the rest of the town. A group of men, carrying ropes and necessary materials, climbed onto the engine. They asked Kate to lead them to where the accident happened. Gladly, she climbed into the cab.

Before long the engine reached the Des Moines River bridge, crossed it much quicker than Kate had earlier, and proceeded on to the Honey Creek bridge. The two stranded men waited on the other side of the river. Kate led the rescue party along the same path around the broken bridge that she'd taken earlier. As dawn broke that next morning, a line was thrown to Ed Wood and he waded out of the water to safety. Then the second man, Adam Agar, was rescued. Kate had saved two men's lives and made sure the passenger train didn't cross the Honey Creek bridge.

Just the Facts

Kate Shelley was born in County Tipperary, Ireland on September 25, 1865. Her father, Michael Shelley, was a section foreman for the Chicago & NorthWestern Railway. He also owned a large farm on the hill over-looking Honey Creek.

Kate's father died December 1, 1878 in Illinois while traveling in a hopeless effort to regain his health. He used all his savings in an attempt to find a cure, and when he died he left his wife and family with only the farm to support them. Kate took over most of the burden of managing the farm.

Kate had two brothers and two sisters. Kate was the oldest, then James, Margaret, Mayme, and John. James drowned, in 1879, while wading alone beneath the railroad bridge spanning the Des Moines River. He didn't know how to swim and had gone in over his head.

The storm that washed out the Honey Creek bridge occurred on July 6, 1881. Kate's actions saved the lives of Ed Wood, engineer, and of Adam Agar, brakeman. Also onboard the ill-fated No. 11 train were A.P. Olmstead, fireman, and Pat Donahue, east section foreman. These two men died as a result of the crash. The body of A.P. Olmstead was never found, despite the efforts of many townspeople searching for him.

Kate's bravery is not diminished by the fact that the railroad had already halted all trains running through the area of the storm. She didn't know that, and risked her life to save those on the trains.

For her courage, many honors and gifts were bestowed on her. The Iowa Legislature presented her with $200 and a gold medal crafted by

Tiffany of New York. On the face of the medal is a raised figure of a girl, carrying a lantern and crossing a railroad bridge. The words Heroism, Youth, and Humanity are engraved around the girl's head. The inscription on the reverse, according to Kate Shelley during a speech she gave in 1888, says:

> *Presented by the State of Iowa, to Kate Shelley, with the thanks of the General Assembly in recognition of the Courage and Devotion of a child of fifteen years whom neither the fury of the elements, nor the fear of death could appal in her effort to save human life during the terrible storm and flood in the Des Moines Valley on the night of July 6th, 1881.*

Kate was invited to speak at many occasions, including at Iowa State College on July 3, 1909 as the college celebrated 50 years at its location in Story County. Miss Frances E. Willard started collecting money to send Kate to college, and raised enough to pay for two terms at Simpson College in Indianola, Iowa during 1883-1884. Unfortunately, Kate had little background in formal education, and thus college life didn't suit her. She returned home to Moingona. She taught school for awhile, as a substitute teacher, but she didn't like that job. However, her two younger sisters, Mayme and Maggie, both taught school for many years.

Next Kate worked as a bill clerk for the Iowa legislature, yet she missed her home along Honey Creek and again returned to live there. In 1888, Kate appeared before a group of people at the Feast of St. John Evangelist to speak on behalf of her family and her desire to save her childhood home from being sold to pay off bills. A Chicago newspaper had a special rug woven and auctioned it off to raise funds to benefit the Shelley family. The newspaper raised in total $917.05 and presented the money to the Shelleys on May 14, 1890. Kate and her family purchased the farm and in June added 17 acres. Then in 1891, they built a new house on the farm to replace the familiar, weather-beaten home.

Kate was living in the new house when another accident occurred on Shelley Curve: early on August 1, 1899, the No. 9 westbound mail train jumped the track, killing four men and injuring seven others. Kate and Mayme arrived on the scene first, and helped the injured until a train was sent from Boone to take the victims to the hospital.

In October 1903, Kate became an agent for the North Western railroad, working at the Moingona station selling tickets and billing freight. When the railroad created a viaduct for the train to use to avoid the 30 bridges along this stretch of track, they named it the Kate Shelley Viaduct. Kate was the only person anywhere who had her own regular stop on a railroad line to board and deboard the train.

Kate never married, though she enjoyed attending dances and socials where she was very popular.

She died from Bright's disease on January 21, 1912. On the day of her funeral, her train picked up her body at her house to take it to Boone for burial at the Sacred Heart Cemetery.

KATE SHELLEY
(The Girl Who Saved The Train)
A true story of heroism in Iowa

By NONY MYLENBUSCH
and RUTH HILE

1. On a lit-tle farm in Io-wa, in the year of eight-y-one, Lived a
2. Near her home there were two bridg-es 'cross the riv-er and the creek; She could

lit-tle girl just fif-teen years of age. On Ju-
hear an en-gine chug-ging on its way. When it

ly sixth, it was storm-ing and the flood-ing had be-gun, And that
crossed the weak-ened tres-tle lead-ing ov-er Hon-ey Creek, With a

night she   heard   the riv - er   in its   rage.
grind -ing   crash   the wood - en bridge gave way.

REFRAIN

KATE SHEL - LEY, KATE SHEL - EY, The Girl Who Saved The Train.   Train.

3. Katy hurried to the rescue, with a lantern in her hand,
   She discovered there was nothing she could do.
   As she saw the battered engine lying buried in the sand,
   She remembered that the night express was due.

4. She-- knew that many people were aboard the speeding train
   And a fatal crash would send them to their grave,
   So she started on her journey nearly blinded by the rain,
   Thinking only of the lives she had to save.

5. She must reach Moingona Station 'bout a mile-- up the track
   And she had to cross the river bridge to go.
   As she crawled upon the trestle, there were chills along her back,
   For-- certain death awaited down below.

6. As she fought her way across the bridge, four hundred feet in length,
   She could feel the timbers swaying to and fro.
   The only thing that saved her was her prayer to God for strength,
   For at times she nearly slipped and fell below.

7. When she finally crawled to safety, though her strength was ebbing fast,
   And her hands were bruised and nails had torn her dress,
   She hurried to the station and her goal was reached at last,
   When the station master flagged the fast express.

8. All the passengers were grateful when Kate Shelley saved the train
   From a certain doom that they could not foresee.
   Though she died in nineteen twelve, her memory is one of fame,
   And her name is written down in history.

Jack Shelley, News Manager of WHO
is a nephew of Kate Shelley.

Winona (Nony Mylenbusch) Decker presented Mamie Eisenhower with a tape of the Kate Shelley Song in 1956 as a gift. Mrs. Eisenhower wrote in a thank you note, "Your gift is one which will be especially prized by our family since it is a recording of one of your own compositions which you have interpreted on the piano." Used by permission.

Check It Out!

Fiction

Porter, Wesley. *Kate Shelley and the Midnight Express: American Folk Legend*. New York: F. Watts, 1979.

San Souci, Robert D. *Kate Shelley: Bound for Legend*. New York: Dial Books for Young Readers, 1995.

Wetterer, Margaret K. *Kate Shelley and the Midnight Express*. Minneapolis: Carolrhoda Books, 1990. (Also available in video format.)

Nonfiction

For the most reliable information on Kate, contact the Boone County Historical Society, 602 Story Street, Boone, Iowa 50036. Phone: 515-432-1907.

Meyers, Edward H. "The Girl They Stopped the Trains For." 42-48. *Trains: The Magazine of Railroading*. October, 1957.

Online Resources

The Ames Public Library has several photos of Kate available for viewing at *http://www.ames.lib.ia.us/farwell/publication/Pub8684.htm*.

Toastmasters member Bill Baxter gave an award-winning speech about Kate. You can read it at *http://www.foundersdistrict.org/Speeches/great_legend.htm*.

Renowned artist P. Buckley Moss created a picture called the Kate Shelley Bridge. To see the picture, and perhaps to order a copy, go to *http://p-buckley-moss.com/thekateshellybridge.html*.

Over the years, several individuals have created personal home pages about Kate. You can learn a bit more about the railroad surrounding the incident at *http://showcase.netins.net/web/bikebarn/rail/kate_shelley.html.*

Wait 'Til You See This!

The Kate Shelley High Bridge spans the Des Moines River northwest of Boone, Iowa. Renamed after Kate Shelley in 1982, it is the longest, highest double-track railroad bridge in the United States. The bridge is 2,685 feet long and 185 feet above the Des Moines River. Contact the Boone Area Chamber of Commerce for more information. 806 Seventh Street, Boone, IA 50036. 1-800-266-6312.

The memorial plaque at Kate's grave. Courtesy Boone Historical Society.

In Moingona, Iowa, you can visit the Kate Shelley Railroad Museum. The museum houses artifacts of Kate's life, a working telegraph system, railroad memorabilia, and a recreated 19th century railroad passenger station. It is open June-September, on Sundays only, from 1–5 p.m. Individual admission is free; a donation is requested from groups. You can make an appointment for other times, or to arrange group tours, by calling 515-432-3342.

Kate Shelley is buried at the Sacred Heart Cemetery, in Boone, Iowa.

Other Sources

Sherr, Lynn and Jurate Kazickas. *Susan B. Anthony Slept Here: A Guide to American Women's Landmarks*. 152. New York: Random House, 1994.

SOPHIE BELL WRIGHT

1881

Teaching to Help Others

Sophie heard the knock on her mother's front door in the little house in New Orleans, but paused a moment to check one of her student's work. Learning was more important than any interruption. The school day was almost complete; whoever it was would wait.

"Watch the alignment of your numbers," Sophie said, pointing at one girl's paper. The rows of numbers mingled until Sophie had difficulty sorting them out. "Your sums are correct, now just work on your neatness."

"Yes, Miss Sophie," Jan said, concentrating once more on her work.

Sophie leaned on her cane and scanned the room of girls, sitting on her mother's upholstered chairs and sofa, each intent on their tasks. Her mother's front parlor had become a school five years earlier when Sophie was 14 years old and needed to help support the family. She had tried to find a job teaching at the local schools, but found that her grammar school diploma wasn't enough. When that attempt failed, she and her sister, Jenny, started a "select school for girls." Charging each girl 50 cents per month brought in a little extra money to help pay for food and clothing. Teaching the girls brought Sophie immense satisfaction and pleasure.

After a few years of running her school, she realized she needed to know more in order to continue as a teacher. Taking her courage in hand, she convinced the principal of the Normal School (a school for teachers) that she could teach math in exchange for auditing language classes. The exchange had proven successful and her little school had flourished.

Now, content that all the students were busy, Sophie smoothed down her skirt with one hand as she limped to the door. Swinging it open, she saw a muscular young man standing on the front step. He held his hat in front of him with both hands, the top becoming a spinning blur as he nervously turned it.

"May I help you?" Sophie asked.

"Miss Sophie?" the man asked. "I hear you run a school and are a great teacher."

Sophie saw his eyes light on the hand holding her cane. The cane head was snuggled into her skirts, with the tip just visible by her feet. Despite having been crippled most of her life, she was still sensitive to the looks of strangers. She knew he must be thinking her too young at 19 years old to have nearly white hair. And of course, the heavy brace she wore made her slight body appear rigid. She straightened her back and gripped her cane more firmly.

"I run a school here, yes. As for being a great teacher, I do my best, but the student must desire to learn in order to be taught."

"Well, Miss, I need to learn. I was a circus acrobat, but now I need to support my family. I have no money to pay you right now, but I'm told you might be able to help me?"

Sophie raised her chin at the thought of having a man mingle with the young girls in her parlor, studying books, writing sums. The parents would never tolerate such a situation. And he had no money. Yet something about him appealed to her. She peered at the man more closely and saw the hope in his eyes. He seemed sincere in his desire to learn. Perhaps....

"I'm sorry I can't help you now," Sophie said. The light in his eyes dimmed at her words. "However, if you'd be willing to come after supper, I can teach you then."

"Thank you, miss!" The man's eyes shone. "Thank you! I'll be here."
With a wave of his hand, the young man strode down the tree-lined street
into the afternoon, almost skipping in his hurry.

Sophie sighed and turned back inside. Another pupil, and this one in
the evening. She would teach him so he could feel proud of himself, support his family, and live a rewarding life. What would she teach? Where
would she start? Did she have the strength to work day and night?

Thoughts whirled in her mind as she stood in the doorway of the parlor, not seeing the students themselves, but looking back in time.

As far back as she could remember she had been crippled. She had
fallen when she was three years old and hurt her back and hip. Her family
had little money for medical treatments, so recovery was slow. She could-
n't walk, and thus sat strapped into a chair. Six long years later, she managed to use a brace and crutches to help her stand and walk. She began
grammar school where she learned about books and numbers. She loved
working with numbers and her teachers said she had a natural talent. Her
handicap proved to be a daily struggle for her, but her determination to
learn was stronger. She'd never forget the sad expression on her father's
face as he told her she had to stop going to school and earn some money
to help keep the family together.

"Miss Sophie?" Jan asked quietly.

Sophie focused once more on the parlor full of girls. She cleared her
thoughts and smiled at the girl. "Yes, Jan?"

"Are we finished for the day? My pa is expecting me."

Sophie glanced at the clock on the mantel over the working fireplace.
"Yes, that will do for today. Remember your homework. I'll be particularly
interested in neatness tomorrow."

Jan blushed, stacking her books. "Yes, ma'am."

Just after sunset, Sophie heard a knock at the front door. She finished her
bite of supper as her sister pushed back from the table and went to answer it.
Sophie watched her sister's straight back leave the dining room, and longed to
be able to walk gracefully. Jenny was taller, attractive, and whole.

"Sophie, you have a student," Jenny said, emerging from the front hall.

Sophie mentally shook herself, banishing the moment of self-pity. She couldn't afford the luxury of wishing to be different than she was. God had dealt this hand for her, and she would play it to the best of her ability.

Sophie's statue in Sophie B. Wright Place, New Orleans, Louisiana. Photo by Chris Bolté.

She carefully rose from her chair, grasped her cane, and walked into the parlor. The young former acrobat reached out to shake her hand as she approached.

"Miss Sophie, you don't know how much this means to me," he said, eyes reflecting the huge smile on his face. "I was telling my buddies at work about you teaching me, and there's a bunch of 'em that want to come also. They's waiting outside. Is it all right for them to learn too?"

"More? How many more?" Sophie asked.

Jenny glanced at her but didn't say anything.

"Ten tonight, but there are several fellas who couldn't come this evening. They had to clear it with their missus."

Sophie surveyed the parlor, counting seats. How many men were there in the city who wanted to learn? Really, the number of seats wasn't an issue—learning could be done on the floor if need be, she decided.

"All right. Ask your friends in," she said.

The men trooped in and filled the small room. They sat on chairs, the sofa, the steps, the floor. Each night Sophie found more men crowding into her parlor, eager to learn so they could find better, high-paying jobs. Sophie taught as many men as would fit in her mother's parlor, but each night there were more men, and each night men were turned away. One evening she turned away several hundred willing students.

She knew something had to be done to accommodate all these men and boys who worked during the day and yet needed schooling in order to make something better of their lives.

"Jenny, I can't keep turning these men away," she said one evening at dinner in 1897. The night school had been successful for twelve years, and showed no signs of dying out. The need persisted for a night school for working men. "Surely we can find a way to teach more men at a time."

"Maybe you could start charging the students," Jenny suggested, "then you could afford to rent a building. Or maybe the school would let you use their classrooms for a small fee."

"These men don't have any extra money. They work hard all day and come to me at night to learn. They sit on the steps with their scraps of paper and write with stubby pencils. I couldn't possibly charge them. No, there must be another way."

Sophie thought about options, and finally decided to ask the wealthier citizens of New Orleans for assistance. She received more help than she'd thought possible. Several citizens put up enough money to build a school and pay for books and desks. Sophie cried the night she opened the new school building for her students.

Now she knew the men would always have a place to learn. And it all started with a simple request from a stranded acrobat.

Just the Facts

Sophie Bell Wright was born in New Orleans, Louisiana, on June 5, 1866, into a family that lost everything during the Civil War.

When Sophie was three, she fell and severely injured her back and hip. She was strapped into a chair for six (some sources say 10) years. Finally, she was able to walk using a brace and a cane. She went to school and received a grammar school education before family finances dictated that she help earn money to support the family. She tried to find a job as a teacher. When that failed, in 1881 she started her own "select school for girls" in her mother's living room. Sophie was 15 years old. She had a sister named Jenny, who also taught in the girls' school. The school became known as the Home Institute and continued in operation until 1928.

In 1885, a stranded acrobat pleaded with her to teach him. She agreed to teach him at night, and that idea blossomed into New Orleans' first free night school. (Sophie did not originate the idea; Dr. J. P. Picton had suggested it in 1845.) The night school operated until 1909 when New Orleans opened a night school of its own. By then, Sophie's school had taught more than 20,000 men and boys.

Sophie was known as a tiny tyrant. She is reported to have said once to a large youngster, "I'm here to teach, not to trifle. Behave yourself, or I'll put your head right through that window."

Sophie spent her entire life teaching and helping others. She was president of the Home for Incurables from December 9, 1908 until her death. She helped raise funds to build an additional wing to care for crippled children. She campaigned for Rest Awhile, a vacation home for working women and children. She also held state and national offices in the benevolent order of King's Daughters and Sons. She served on the Executive Board of the National Federation of Women's Clubs, and was an honorary vice president of the National Congress of Mothers.

In 1903, the Progressive Union chose her to receive *The Times-Picayune* Loving Cup for her kind and generous spirit. Sophie was the first woman to receive the Cup, and only the third person. The residents of New Orleans showed their appreciation for her efforts when they presented her with a $10,000 check to pay off the mortgage she'd placed on her home and school to sustain her charitable works.

In 1911, she was honored to have a new public school named for her. The Sophie B. Wright Girls' High School was dedicated on April 9, 1912.

Sophie's school continues to educate students in New Orleans. Photo by Chris Bolté.

Sophie died on June 10, 1912, just two months after the dedication. She said to her doctor, before dying, "Say good-bye to my girls for me." She was 46 years old. Sophie was buried in Metaire Cemetery in New Orleans.

A group of caring residents and business owners in the Garden and Lower Garden districts of New Orleans collected money to erect a statue to Sophie. In April 1988, Mexican artist Enrique Alferez created a bronze sculpture of Sophie, which was erected in Sophie B. Wright Place.

Check It Out!

Gehman, Mary and Nancy Ries. *Women and New Orleans: A History.* New Orleans: Margaret Media, Inc, 1988. Fourth Printing, 1996.

Online Resources

The New Orleans Public Library owns several rare printed materials pertaining to Sophie. Go to *http://home.gnofn.org/~nopl/spec/speclist.htm*. Click on the link to their "Index to the Rare Vertical File," then scroll down to "Wright, Sophie B." The files are open only to "Registered Louisiana Division researchers" so you'll need to contact an Archivist at the library for assistance.

Louisiana has created an online timeline of historic events. You can learn more about Sophie by going to their Web site: *http://www.enlou.com/time/year1885.htm*.

Sophie is called an "Educator and Social Reformer" by the Louisiana State University. Go to *http://indigo.lib.lsu.edu/soc/women/lawomen/wright.html*.

Wait 'Til You See This!

Sophie B. Wright Place is located at the junction of Magazine and St. Andrew streets. A bronze sculpture of Sophie stands at one end of the small park.

Sophie B. Wright Middle School is located at 1426 Napoleon Avenue, New Orleans, Louisiana.

Other Sources

Sherr, Lynn and Jurate Kazickas. *Susan B. Anthony Slept Here: A Guide to American Women's Landmarks*. 169. New York: Random House, 1994.

Minnie Freeman

1888

Minnie's Promise

Minnie looked up from the book on her wooden desk and glanced out the window of the sod schoolhouse. Another blast of wind rattled the glass. She knew a blizzard was coming. She had lived in Nebraska long enough to recognize the signs. The unusually warm January morning had coaxed the children before class started to play outside without their coats. Now the wind blew from the north and brought a sudden drop in the temperature along with it. They had already stoked the fire with more coal to ward off the freezing temperatures outside. Minnie knew they had enough coal to see them through the night, if necessary. She'd rather the children return home to their families, though.

She scanned the 17 students seated at their desks, heads bent over their work, though a head occasionally turned toward the window. About half of them were teenagers who had grown up on the prairie. They knew as well as she did what was coming.

"Children," Minnie said. "We're going to have a blizzard. I'm dismissing class for today. Please gather your things and dress warmly for the walk home."

Minnie and her students in front of the sod schoolhouse. Courtesy Nebraska State Historical Society.

A scramble of feet followed, with the older children helping the younger children wrap up as well as they could in their cloaks and overcoats. The raging wind became white with snowflakes hurling past the window.

"Hurry, now. The storm is growing worse." Minnie fastened the last hook on one little girl's cloak as she spoke. "Do not be frightened. You will reach home safely, I'm sure."

Suddenly a squall of wind struck the windows harder than before and the panes gave way, crashing to the floor of the schoolhouse. The door blew off its hinges and skidded across the floor. The younger children screamed. A rush of snow and ice whirled in, creating drifts across the plank floor. Two older boys grabbed the door and fastened it in place, but the windows were still open and snow piled up inside the one-room school. Minnie realized the children would not be safe for long. Their best chance was to try to get to the boarding house where Minnie stayed, about a mile away. Quickly, she grabbed a ball of twine from her desk and tied each child's wrist to the next in a line, then fastened the end to her own wrist. She talked quietly to the children, trying to keep them calm as they waited to see what would happen next.

She was glad her students liked and trusted her, despite the fact that she wasn't much older than some of them. She had grown up in Ord, Nebraska and gone to school at York College. Now at the age of 19 she was the teacher at Midvale school in Mira Valley. And the lives of her seventeen pupils were tied to her wrist.

The wind moaned outside as the snow swirled. Then the moan grew louder as the roof suddenly lifted from the sod walls and blew away. Snow blew more fiercely into the open schoolhouse.

They could not stay at the school and survive the storm. If they could reach the boarding house, then they could wait it out. There were food and warmth there.

"Come on, children," she said, and led the way out an open window frame.

Ice and snow pelted her face, and she could barely see where she was heading. Wind roared in her ears. The sky had darkened with the thickness of the snow clouds. Minnie struggled on, pulling the line of students behind her. Occasionally, she could feel a tug on the twine as someone behind slipped in the snow or had trouble stomping through the deepening drifts. She didn't try to talk to the student behind her, rather motioned with her hand to provide direction and comfort. Minnie knew they must keep moving if they were to have any chance of reaching the house.

Minnie Freeman. Courtesy Nebraska State Historical Society.

With each step Minnie took, she hoped and prayed that God would see them all safely into the warmth of the farmhouse. Her energy waned, leaving only her determination to propel her onward. She hoped they were walking in the right direction and not becoming confused by the swirling of snowflakes in front of their eyes. The responsibility of the lives behind her weighed heavy on her mind, and pushed her forward despite her own fatigue and fear, as they fought their way through the storm.

Suddenly, her feet slipped out from under her and she plunged into the snow. She was so tired. She almost wanted to just stay and rest a while. She shook her head. That was certain death. She looked at her students, their worried frowns showing their concern. Several hands reached out and helped her up. She brushed snow from her face and squared her shoulders. She would see them through this. She plodded on, one step in front of the other, her head bowed against the fierce wind.

Minnie raised her head against the blinding snow and could barely discern a lantern in the window of the farmhouse ahead. Almost there. With renewed energy, she kept walking, leading the trusting children behind her. Finally they reached the door. Minnie pushed it open and light and heat rushed out to meet the snow blowing in.

"Minnie! What's this?" the housewife who ran the boarding house cried, hurrying to the door.

Minnie ushered the children in before closing the door securely against the wind. They'd made it to safety, food, and warmth, just as she'd promised.

Just the Facts

Minnie Mae Freeman was born in Ord, Nebraska in 1869. She attended York College and then started teaching at the Midvale school. She was 19 years old when the blizzard hit on January 12, 1888. The actual count of the number of people who died during the storm varies widely from 40 to 100 for Nebraska alone. With the help of her older students, Minnie led her class to the boarding house nearly a mile away.

She is described as:

slightly above the medium height, has dark brown hair, gray eyes, and is rather pretty.... She is an accomplished young lady in every particular. She is an artist and has done some good work both in crayon and oil, and is also a good musician.

One student who walked with Minnie to safety later became Mrs. Ben Eberhart of Valley county. In W. H. O'Gara's book, *In All Its Fury,* she recalled years after the blizzard "how very reluctant they were to leave the rest of the pupils who were having such a jolly time at the teacher's boarding place." Minnie told how she helped the housewife cook a meal that would feed the hungry crowd of children.

Minnie's rescue of her students came to symbolize what other teachers had done during the storm. Newspapers across the country told of her heroic deed. Minnie didn't see it as heroic or unusual, rather her act was merely in the line of duty. She wrote a letter to a friend (as quoted in one 1888 edition of *Household Companion*) describing her role in the event. At the end of her letter she said: "Now that is all there is to it, and I really do not think that I am deserving of so much credit." Her attitude endeared her to the reading public. She was given a gold watch and chain by Mr. Andrews of San Francisco, California. She also received many letters of congratulations, and a gold medal from the State Board of Education.

An admirer of hers, Mrs. Ellis of St. Paul, Nebraska, wrote the following acrostic poem in her honor. Note how the first letter of each line, when put together, spells "Minnie Freeman Saint Paul."

'Midst driving winds and blinding snows,
Impending dangers round her close;
No shelter from the blast and sleet,
No earthly help to guide her feet.
In God alone she puts her trust,
Ever to guide the brave and just.

Fierce and loud the awful storm,
Racking now her slender form,
Eager to save the little band
Entrusted to her guiding hand.
Marshalled her host, see, forth she goes
And falters not while tempest blows;
Now God alone can help, she knows.

See them falling as they go;
Angry winds around them blow.
Is there none to hear their cry?
Now her strength will almost fail;
Tranquil, she braves the fearful gail.

Preëminent her name shall stand,
A beacon light o'er all the land,
Unrivalled on the page of time;
Let song and story swell the chime.

She later married E. B. Penney and moved to Fullerton, Nebraska.

Check It Out!

"The Blizzard of 1888." *Nebraska Pioneer Reminiscences.* 203-5. Chapter written by Minnie Freeman Penney.

O'Gara, W. H. *In All Its Fury: A History of the Blizzard of January 12, 1888.* Lincoln: Union College Press. Published by The January 12, 1888 Blizzard Club.

Wait 'Til You See This!

An historical marker stands on Highway 70, in Valley County, south of Ord, Nebraska. The marker was erected by the now-dissolved January 12, 1888 Blizzard Club, and the Historical Land Mark Council. In part, the text of the marker reads: "On January 12, 1888, a sudden fierce blizzard slashed across the Midwest. The temperature fell to between 30 and 40 degrees below zero....The story of Minnie Freeman has become symbolic of these many acts of heroism."

Other Sources

Alter, Judith. "Teacher, Doctor, Lawyer." *Women of the Old West*. New York: Franklin Watts, 1989.

Bowen, Ezra. "At 100, still the champ of winter's snowy Olympics; the blizzards of 1888." *Smithsonian*. Vol 18, No. 12, 70. Wash., DC: Smithsonian Institution, March 1988.

Creigh, Dorothy Weyer. "The Homesteaders." *Nebraska: A Bicentennial History*. New York: W.W. Norton & Company, Inc., 1977.

Hickey, Donald R. "The Blizzard of '88." *Nebraska Moments: Glimpses of Nebraska's Past*. 146-151. Lincoln: Univ of Nebraska Press.

Historical marker text provided by the Nebraska State Historical Society.

Letter written by Minnie Mae Freeman to her friend Anna, dated November 17, 1887.

Nebraska Women through the years: 1867-1967. A record of the feminine contribution to the winning of the west. Johnsen Publishing Co., 1967.

"Our Portrait Gallery: Minnie Mae Freeman." *Household Companion.* 1888.

Sherr, Lynn and Jurate Kazickas. *Susan B. Anthony Slept Here: A Guide to American Women's Landmarks.* 268. New York: Random House, 1994.

EDWINA FAY FULLER

1890

Conquering Mt. Rainier

Fay halted her horse and surveyed the beautiful clearing. The green lushness of Mount Rainier surrounded her, while a stream chuckled nearby. Tall cedars and fir trees framed the view of distant mountain peaks. Clouds drifted past, alternately hiding and revealing the snow-capped scene.

Dismounting from her horse, she was glad that no old-fashioned nosey women were around to make a fuss about her riding like a man, or about the "immodest" clothes she wore. She opened the coatdress to let in some cool air, and straightened the legs of the blue flannel bloomers that reached to her ankles. Then she brushed back wisps of blonde hair that had escaped from her bun, and made sure her straw hat remained securely in place.

"Are you ready, then?" Len Longmire walked up beside her.

Was she ready? She'd waited three years for the chance to climb all the way to the top of the 14,410 foot high mountain. She had made sure she was fit and strong enough for the climb by working out with the Women's Guard, doing calisthenics and rifle drills, despite the locals' shock at the unfeminine activity. She also had listened whenever anyone talked about climbing and waited for her chance. Then a new friend, Philemon Van Trump, suggested she might like to join his family on their outing to the mountain. Fay realized when she saw Philemon had brought his daughter Christine, only eleven years old, that the group would not climb to the top. Somehow Fay knew then that she would find a way.

Fay smiled at Len, lifting her square chin. "Yes, I am ready," she said.

The group crossed the Nisqually River bridge, near the foot of the Nisqually glacier. Len and his father had recently built the bridge so the crossing was much easier than the last time she'd come up the mountain. After everyone readjusted their packs, the group climbed a steep hill on foot. The heavy calfskin shoes that Fay wore over her wool stockings cushioned her feet along the trail. She'd bought boys' shoes instead of trying to make do with the flimsier women's shoes that were available. After an hour of hiking, they came to a clearing that to Fay looked like paradise. Green grass spread before her, dotted with fir trees and many kinds of wildflowers. All the preparations had been well worth the effort.

"Let's set up camp over there at Camp of the Clouds," Len said. He led the way and soon everyone was ready to fix supper and then settle in for the night.

Stars twinkled overhead as Fay let her mind envision the coming days. Although she loved riding horses, she was glad the three days of riding were behind them. Now the real challenge would begin. Could she be the first woman to climb Mt. Rainier? She knew in her heart she could do it. If only she could find a hiking party that was headed to the top.

Fay Fuller shortly after her climb. Courtesy Washington State Historical Society.

The next morning the group gathered some of the wildflowers, pressed them for their collections, and set up a comfortable camp. Before long, another climbing party from Seattle hiked past and set up their camp about 500 feet higher than theirs. Fay decided the time had come.

She and Len hiked up the hill. After introducing herself, she visited with them for a while. Several members of the party planned to try to reach the summit and talked about how they would go about it. Finally, Fay heard the words she'd waited for.

"Would you like to join us?" one of the men asked.

"Yes, I would," she said, smiling.

The others in the group were young and adventurous like Fay. The party's leader was Reverend Ernest C. Smith, who at age 24 had just become the Unitarian minister in Seattle. A photographer, William Amsden, wanted to take pictures at the top of the mountain with his cumbersome 8x10 camera and glass lenses. Robert R. Parrish wanted to conquer Mt. Rainier so much he'd traveled from Portland, Oregon to Yelm, Washington to make the attempt. And of course, Len Longmire from Tacoma, Washington.

Fay returned to the Camp of the Clouds and packed her things. Her food supplies included beef, ham, cold boiled eggs, sardines, bread and butter, cheese, chocolate, dried fruits, brandy and a flask of whiskey. She also carried her alpenstock (hiking stick), which had been made from a curved shovel handle by a blacksmith in Yelm. Then she climbed back up to join the other party for the night before leaving the next morning. She could only hope her mother would understand her sleeping in a camp with all men, and no chaperone.

The morning of August 9, 1890 found the small group heading out wearing their goggles and dark veils to protect them from the bright sun on the snow. They had enough provisions to camp out on the snow for as long as three days if necessary. Fay's heart beat harder as they climbed closer to her goal that day.

After lunch, they kept climbing. Suddenly Ernest Smith realized that the ground glass he carried with him to focus his camera had broken.

"I think I have enough pieces to focus," he said. "At least, I hope so."

They stopped long enough for Smith to take photographs of the mountains stretched before them from the site known as Camp Muir. Then they walked on, step by step going higher up the mountain.

"Oh, no!" Smith cried.

Fay turned around and looked back at where Smith was examining his three-foot mercury barometer. "What's wrong?"

"It's broken," he said. "I guess now all I can do is enjoy the rest of the trip." He smiled ruefully at her.

Fay nodded, uncertain what to say to make him feel better. At least he was taking his losses well. She started hiking up the slope before her. As they reached a particularly dangerous area, Robert Parrish threw his pack up to safe ground before making the attempt to follow it. He gasped as the pack missed and bounced its way down the crevasse. The loss of his provisions and supplies could prove to be a danger to them all.

Before long they stopped and set up camp for the night, glad that no more accidents had happened. They stuck their alpenstocks into the ground and stretched their tents over them for a shelter. After eating dinner, they settled in for a long, cold night that didn't let them sleep much.

When they awoke on August 10, they found the stream had frozen over and their canteens were empty. Fay had only a bit of chocolate with a few raisins and prunes for breakfast before they began to climb once again.

Like the stream, the trails were covered with ice, making walking across ledges and slippery slopes difficult and tiring. At one point they reach a 50-foot stretch of ice they had to cross. Ernest Smith, using his hatchet, cut steps into the ice to reach the other side. Fay struggled and sweated in her long coat with full skirt to use the steps cut for a man's stride.

When they reached a particularly bad place, one of the men reached out a hand to help Fay across.

"No thanks," she said. "I want to get up there under my own power or not at all."

The frozen trail grew worse as the day progressed. When they reached the worst crossing at a high cliff known as Gibraltar, Fay's companions suggested they could tie a rope to her and connect it to two men in front and in back to help her across. The ice holding the rocks together would soon melt as the sun climbed higher in the sky, making the crossing even more dangerous. After considering the risks, Fay agreed, though reluctantly. She wanted to reach the top and nothing, not even herself, would stand in her way.

The higher they climbed, the thinner the air became. Fay found it more and more difficult to climb. She, like the others, could only take a few steps before resting, then a few more. She noticed that the men's mustaches were frozen. But she could see the top now, and it wasn't too much farther. A few steps, rest, a few steps. Finally the group reached the summit of Mt. Rainier.

Fay gazed at the breathtaking vista before her. Snow-covered mountain peaks rose while valleys fell down to rivers. Birds soared, some playing in warm updrafts of air that allowed them to hang motionless in the sky. She couldn't find words powerful enough to describe what she saw and felt as she stood on the crest, while the wind roared past her and clouds hung to one side so she couldn't see what lay beyond them. She had made it to the top! The numbing cold, fatigue, sunburn blisters on her face, the hunger and thirst had all been worth it. She breathed deeply, enjoying her victory.

Now the air was cooling as evening approached. They camped in a steam cave where they'd be warm for the night, then they would descend the mountain in the morning. As they bedded down, Fay watched the stars and meteors through the vent in the roof. Her companions rubbed their feet with whiskey to keep them warm. She was warm on the side closest to the steam vent, and freezing on the other. Occasionally the splitting and roaring of an avalanche crashing down the mountain woke her.

In the morning, they left a sardine can containing their names, a brandy flask, and a tin cup in a crater near the steam cave, as a marker of their accomplishment. Fay grinned to herself. She'd made it to the top and into the history books.

Just the Facts

Fay Fuller was born in 1870 in the New England states, though no one mentions exactly where or when. Her father was Edward N. Fuller and her mother was Augusta Morrison Fuller. She had one brother, Robert E. Fuller. Her family moved from Chicago to Tacoma, Washington, in 1882 where her father became editor of the *Evening News*. They lived in a house on St. Helens Avenue. Fay graduated from high school in 1885 and began to teach at age 15 at the Longfellow School. She also taught at Rosedale on Henderson Bay, which was a day's trip by steamer from Tacoma.

While teaching was an appropriate career for a woman in those days, Fay didn't always do what was considered ladylike. She exercised with the Women's Guard, and she rode horses astride rather than sidesaddle.

She made her first attempt at climbing the mountain in 1887 at 17 years old. She had to turn back, though, at a pre-determined elevation, which was frustrating for her. She decided someday she would climb to the top. According to several accounts, in 1890 Philemon Van Trump spoke to her students about his climbing of Mt. Rainier, and Fay became friends with him. When he offered to take her on his next climb that August, she was thrilled.

Her equipment for the climb included an alpenstock made by a Yelm blacksmith from a curved shovel handle, with a spike in the end for poking into the ground. She also carried several blankets and wore a charcoal mixture on her face as a suncreen. The charcoal mixture, however, did not protect her. Instead, she suffered from swelling that distorted her face, and painful wrists where the skin peeled off. Her food supplies were dried beef, fried ham, cold boiled eggs, sardines, bread and butter, extract of beef, cheese, chocolate, dried peaches, raisins and prunes, brandy, and a flask of whiskey. As they camped in the ice cave, the combination of cold, exhaustion, and the rotten-egg smell of sulphur made her feel sick.

After returning to Yelm, she wrote an account of her climb for her father's paper. Within that story, she wrote, "It was a heavenly moment. Words cannot describe scenery and beauty, how they could speak for the soul!"

Fay became one of the founding members of the Mazamas Mountain Climbers' club, and after climbing the mountain again in 1897, wrote an article about them for the August 15, 1897 edition of the *Tacoma Ledger*.

Fay was also the first woman reporter for the *Tacoma Ledger*. She covered events throughout the city, requiring her to walk miles through dust and mud. She worked for the newspapers in Pendleton, Oregon, as well. She went to Chicago and St. Louis to write about the world's fairs held there. And eventually she went to Washington, D.C., to work.

Fay married Fritz von Briesen in June 1905 in New York City. He was an 1895 Harvard graduate and was a patent and trademark attorney. They lived on West 57th Street in New York for many years. They had two children: Hans von Briesen and a daughter whose name is reported only as Mrs. Edward Neuhauser of Boston. Fay and Fritz's children gave them seven grandchildren.

Edwina Fay Fuller von Briesen died in Santa Monica, California, on May 27, 1958 at the age of 88 years old.

On August 10, 1990, 33 women, under the guidance of the Northwest Chapter of Woodswomen and Women Climbers of the Northwest, climbed Mt. Rainier to mark the 100 year anniversary of Fay Fuller's accomplishment.

Check It Out!

Molenaar, Dee. *The Challenge of Rainier*. Seattle: The Mountaineers, 1979.

Potts, Betsy. "Fay Fuller: First Woman to the Top of Mount Rainier." *Columbia Magazine*. Winter 1996-97.

Write to the Washington State Historical Society, Research Center, 315 North Stadium Way, Tacoma, WA 98403, for copies of related articles.

Online Resources

The Mazamas Mountain Climbers club, founded in 1894, can be reached at *www.mazamas.org*.

For information on Mount Rainier, go to *www.nsp.gov* and select "Visit the Parks" for a list of the national park homepages.

Wait 'Til You See This!

You can hike to the top of Mt. Rainier by going to Mount Rainier National Park. Fay Peak, named after Fay Fuller, overlooks Mowich Lake in the Northwestern part of the park.

Other Sources

Duncan, Don. "The Mountain–The Majestic Bulk of Mount Rainier Looms as a Symbol of the Northwest." *The Seattle Times*. June 20, 1993. Travel section, K1.

Duncan, Don. "Because She Was There – A century later 33 women commemorate a high mark in honor of Tacoma climber." *The Seattle Times*. August 9, 1990. Scene section, D1.

"Famous Reporter's Son Visits Tacoma." *The Tacoma News Tribune*. December 9, 1957.

"Fay Fuller." *Notable Women*. [full citation unavailable]

"First Woman to Conquer Mountain Dies." [Tacoma News Tribune(?)] May 27, 1958.

Kellogg, Caroline. "Bloomer-clad Fay Fuller's trek shocked Tacoma." [Time Machine(?)] Date unknown.

Linsley, Jeann. "Not for Men Only – Women Commemorate Fuller's Historic Ascent." *The Seattle Times.* August 10, 1990. Sports section, C6.

"She Climbed Mt. Tacoma Despite Clothes Handicap Way Back in Gay Nineties." [*Tacoma Ledger*(?)] May 25, 1930.

Sherr, Lynn and Jurate Kazickas. *Susan B. Anthony Slept Here: A Guide to American Women's Landmarks.* 472. New York: Random House, 1994.

Smoot, Jeff. *Adventure Guide to Mount Rainier.* Evergreen: Chockstone Press, 1991.

Whitney, Marci. "First woman to climb Rainier." *The Tacoma News Tribune.* February 15, 1976. E3.

LUCILLE MULHALL

1899

World's First Famous Cowgirl

Lucille pulled on her worn leather gloves as she watched the scene before her. Longhorn cattle milled nervously about in the holding pen at one side of a huge empty field. Occasionally one would sound off to the crowd of spectators gathered behind a rope fence. Cowboys lounged around, discussing the ongoing roping competition. Lucille settled her brimmed hat on her head more securely, waiting her turn.

"Next up, ladies and gentlemen," the announcer said, "a newcomer to the fair here in St. Louis. He recently won the roping contest at his home-town of Claremore, Oklahoma. Let's see what he can do here today, folks. Will Rogers!"

Lucille stepped closer so she could watch the young cowboy's attempt at roping the longhorn.

Will sat his horse easily, his rope ready. In a second, the steer leapt from the holding pen and raced across the field. His horse galloped after it, dirt flying from beneath pounding hooves. The noise from the audience stand-ing and sitting along the edges of the field grew in appreciation as Will's rope landed effortlessly at the base of the curving horns and tightened abruptly around them. Suddenly the steer pulled hard on the rope in such a way that Will's horse was pulled to the ground. Will hit the ground hard, rolling off to one side and standing up quickly.

Lucille Mulhall
America's Greatest Hoese-Woman
"Calling For Time"

Lucille calling for time. Courtesy Archives & Manuscripts Division of the Oklahoma Historical Society.

"Oh, no!" Lucille cried. She hated to see a competitor hurt.

The crowd gasped as well. Several cowboys ran out to help free the steer and horse from the rope. Will grabbed his hat from the ground, beat it against his leg to shed the dust from it, and walked over to his horse. He took the reins and led the horse off the field, waving his hat to the crowd as they clapped for his escape from injury.

"What a shame! Maybe next time, Will," the announcer said, then he started talking about upcoming events at this 1899 St. Louis county fair.

As he droned on, Lucille realized she was up next. She made her way to her horse, her divided skirt swinging about her patent leather boots. She lived for this moment. The joy of testing her roping skills against the cowboys. She'd been riding and roping since she was a little girl. When she was eight years old, her dad had told her she could have all the cattle she could rope and brand. He soon regretted that offer. Lucille proceeded to make a brand in the shape of her initials—LM—and then roped and branded every steer and cow she could. Finally, Zack called off the deal, saying she'd own all the cattle on the ranch if she continued.

Lucille's hometown of Mulhall was named in honor of Lucille's father, Zack. Photo by Chris Bolté.

Lucille's hair was already damp inside her hat. She concentrated on checking her pony's girth and bridle, ignoring the crowd around her. She swung up onto her saddle, her horse stepping out as soon as she was settled.

Lucille's father had started organizing and managing roping and riding contests earlier in the year. He started The Congress of Rough Riders and Ropers and Lucille performed in roping contests against the cowboys. She also demonstrated trick riding and trick roping. Lucille enjoyed the competitions and loved working with the horses. The Congress had already performed in Oklahoma City, Vinita, and South McAlester, all of which were in the Twin Territories (Oklahoma).

Her hand reached for her rope as she approached the starting line. She tried to stay calm, to not let her shyness show, as she appeared before the large crowd.

"Now, ladies and gentlemen," the announcer went on, "you're in for a special treat. Miss Lucille Mulhall is about to show you how even a fine young lady of 14 years can rope these immense wild animals. Here she is! Miss Lucille Mulhall!"

Lucille ready to perform. Courtesy Archives & Manuscripts Division of the Oklahoma Historical Society. #20630.1.

The crowd clapped and cheered as she positioned her roping pony for the race to catch the steer. The crowd gradually grew quieter, holding its breath, waiting. Lucille sat easily in the saddle, the reins short on her eager pony, one hand holding the lasso ready. Her brimmed hat was pushed securely on her head, her eyes trained on the steer and the man ready to open the gate.

Lucille gave a nod that she was ready. The man opened the gate and jumped back. The steer bolted from the holding pen, running straight across the open field. Lucille clamped her heels into her pony and it leapt forward, galloping after the longhorn. Her pony was well-trained and knew his job. Lucille's lasso spun as the pony neared the animal. Judging the pony's speed along with the longhorn's speed and direction, she aimed the lasso and tossed the loop. The rope snugged down over the long dangerous horns. As soon as the loop landed, the pony slid to a halt and laid back on the rope.

"Good boy!" Lucille cried, as the pony backed up a few steps. The steer flipped onto its side at the sudden jolt of the rope.

"Hold 'em!" she called to her pony. The pony dipped its head slightly as though in answer, and maintained the tension on the rope.

Lucille jumped from the saddle and ran to the steer before it could get back on its feet. She pulled a shorter rope from her waistband and wrapped it quickly around the steer's hooves. She threw both her hands up to stop the timer. The crowd cheered and clapped for the young girl.

"That's the way it oughta be done, folks!" the announcer said. "And almost good enough to take home first prize. We'll see more of this young lady, you can count on that."

Lucille smiled and nodded to the crowd, then walked back to her waiting pony. She'd done her best, even if she didn't win first prize. She mounted and urged it forward, releasing the tension on the rope. After a cowboy pulled the rope off the steer's horns, Lucille wrapped her rope while the steer was herded back to the holding pen by several mounted cowboys.

The competition continued as Lucille led her pony back to its temporary stall. She walked past the now-dusty Will Rogers, as he tended his horse's scrapes. He looked up at her and grinned in embarrassment. Lucille smiled back and halted her pony.

"Tough break," she said. "Your name's Will, right?"

"Yep."

"Is your horse all right?"

This historical marker stands along Main Street in Mulhall, Oklahoma. Photo by Chris Bolté.

The young cowboy straightened up and faced her, laying a hand on his horse's withers as he spoke. "He'll be fine. Thanks for asking."

Lucille nodded. "That could have been much worse. I'm glad you're both okay."

"You had a fine ride." Will pulled his hat from his head as he realized he was speaking to a lady. "You been riding long?"

Lucille laughed. "All my life, it seems."

"Sometimes it feels like I've spent my entire life in the saddle, too," Will said, grinning.

"Well, I've gotta be going," Lucille said. "Nice meeting you."

In the months that followed, Lucille's father took the Congress to many other county fairs in the Midwest. Lucille was glad her new friend, Will, went with them. She laughed at his antics, especially when he pretended to play a trombone in the Cowboy Band. Then, when her father was challenged to have a band member compete against a cowboy, he'd call on Will or another fake band member, Jim O'Donnell, to meet the rodeo challenge. The crowd never seemed to catch on to the ploy, and everyone had a good time. Lucille knew her father used very creative means to draw crowds to his shows. It was part of his charm.

On July 4, 1900, the Congress accepted an invitation to perform at a reunion of Theodore Roosevelt's Rough Riders in Oklahoma City. Teddy Roosevelt was running for Vice President of the United States and was glad to have a chance to campaign in the Oklahoma Territory. Having a reunion with his former comrades was an added bonus.

The Cowboy band performed several songs, entertaining the large audience. Lucille performed as usual—roping longhorn cattle, trick roping, and trick riding. After Lucille's performance, Teddy Roosevelt approached her father, Zack.

"Mr. Mulhall," Roosevelt said, shaking Zack's hand. "You have a remarkable young lady for a daughter."

"Thank you, sir," Zack said, smiling.

"With such skills," Roosevelt went on, "you should take this wonderful girl all over America and let everyone see her."

"That's not a bad idea, sir," Zack said. "I just might do that."

Lucille grinned at her father. She'd like nothing better than to be with her dad, traveling the country, riding horses and performing—a real Cowgirl. She could get used to that.

Just the Facts

Lucille Mulhall was born in St. Louis, Missouri on October 21, 1885. Her parents were Colonel Zach Mulhall and Mary Agnes Mulhall. Mary Agnes died January 1931, at the age of 78.

Lucille Mulhall. Courtesy Archives & Manuscripts Division of the Oklahoma Historical Society.

Lucille had two brothers and three sisters: Logan, Marmaduke, twins Mildred and Madolyn, and Agnes. She also had two adopted siblings, Mildred and Charley, whose parents were Zach and his mistress, Georgia.

She moved (at the age of four) with her family from St. Louis, Missouri, to a ranch near Alfred, Oklahoma (later renamed Mulhall in honor of Zack). She grew up among roping and branding, bronco busting, and shooting rattlesnakes. She competed against men in a man's sport and won, yet kept her femininity and morals intact. Hailed by Will Rogers as the first famous cowgirl, she was a champion at steer roping and trick riding.

She had a trick horse named Governor who could do amazing stunts that one newspaper reported (according to Kathryn Stansbury's book *Lucille Mulhall: Wild West Cowgirl*) as "He picks up a handkerchief, goes lame, plays dead, rings a bell, takes off his mistress' hat, walks on his knees, picks up a whip, and sits on his haunches and crosses his forelegs." He became almost as famous as Lucille.

One of her best roping achievements happened when she was 20, during a competition for the best average roping time of three steers, held at Coffeyville, Kansas, in September 1905. Her first time was 32 seconds, her second 40, and her third 42. She won $1000 and became Champion Steer Roper.

Lucille helped open the doors for other girls and women to compete in rodeos, by being better than her male competitors.

Her life was downright difficult. Sleeping in a tent or a boxcar took some getting used to at first for the young woman. Her devotion to her father, Zack, and to her career showed its effect in the failure of two marriages in short periods of time. She married Martin Van Bergen in 1907, keeping it a secret for a year from her family.

They had a son, William Logan Van Bergen, who was born January 29, 1909. But Lucille didn't hang around to raise him. She was off again with her family to perform, this time at the 101 Ranch Real Wild West show at Ponca City, Oklahoma, the same year. The little baby was left with her husband's parents to be cared for. She only saw her son a few times before she divorced Martin in March of 1914. She later married Tom Burnett, a Texan and rancher, but that relationship soon broke up as well. There were rumors of other romances, and possibly weddings, with Bud Ballew and J.W. McCormick.

Lucille continued riding for many years after the breakup of her dad's wild west show. She performed on vaudeville stages with her trick horse Governor and others, and finally retired to the open range of her home in Mulhall, Oklahoma.

In April 1935, Lucille was invited to lead a parade on horseback with Pawnee Bill (a.k.a. Gordon Lillie) in the town of Guthrie, Oklahoma. The town was celebrating '89er day. She wore her traditional costume—a beaded jacket over a white shirt and a red skirt that reached below her boot tops—as she rode a horse down the street. The *Daily Oklahoman* called her the "'most fearless and intrepid' horsewoman in the world."

Her last public performance was in September 1940, when she was an honored guest at the Cherokee Strip Parade in Ponca City, Oklahoma.

The Mulhall family grave marker at Roselawn Cemetery. Photo by Betty Bolté.

She died December 21, 1940, at the age of 55, in a car accident a mile from the ranch. She was buried in the family mausoleum on the ranch. In 1946, her family moved all the caskets of the Mulhall family to Roselawn Cemetery. In 1985, Lucille's nieces Martha Fisch and Virginia Pennington, along with Charley's widow Esther, added a tombstone to the formerly unmarked family plot.

Check It Out!

Fiction

Alter, Judy. *Cherokee Rose: A Novel of America's First Cowgirl.* New York: Bantam Books, 1996.

Nonfiction

Romulo, Beth Day. *America's First Cowgirl, Lucille Mulhall.* New York: Julian Messner, Inc., 1955.

Stansbury, Kathryn B. *Lucille Mulhall: Wild West Cowgirl.* Second Edition, Revised. Mulhall: Homestead Heirlooms Pub Co., 1992.

Online Resources

You can see pictures of many famous cowgirls, including Lucille, and access other related links, at *www.cowgirls.com/dream/cowgals/mulhall.htm.*

You can learn more about cowgirls in general, including Lucille, at *http://cyberrodeo.com/guysgals/cg7.htm.*

The Mining Company has a list of related books, including *Cherokee Rose,* which you can purchase. Go to *http://rodeo.miningco.com/library/weekly/aa051197.htm.*

Catherine Lavender has created a Web site dedicated to Western Women's History, called WestWeb. You can find it at *www.library.csi.cuny.edu/west-web/pages/women.html.*

You can request books about Lucille and other famous cowgirls at *www.cowgirls.com/dream/bk_cowgirls.htm.*

Visit the National Cowgirl Hall of Fame Web site at *www.cowgirl.net/.*

Wait 'Til You See This!

The Oklahoma Historical Society has an exhibit that includes the beaded vest given to Lucille by Apache chief Geronimo. For more information on exhibits, contact the Oklahoma Historical Society, Oklahoma Street, Territorial Museum, 402 East Oklahoma, Guthrie, OK 73044-3317. 405-282-1889.

The National Cowgirl Hall of Fame and Western Heritage Center, in Hereford, Texas, has an exhibit of Lucille, the first known female to be called a cowgirl, a term some say was created by Will Rogers. You can also see an exhibit at the Rodeo Hall of Fame, a branch of the National Cowboy Hall of Fame in Oklahoma City.

An historical marker titled "Mulhall: Oklahoma Territory" is located on Main Street in Mulhall, Oklahoma. It reads in part, "Town name was changed June 6, 1890 to honor Zack Mulhall, rancher and Wild West Show Promoter. His daughter, Lucille Mulhall, was famous as 'World's First Cowgirl.'"

Lucille is buried at Roselawn Cemetery, on a hill overlooking the town of Mulhall, Oklahoma.

The Stone Lion Inn, a bed-and-breakfast in Guthrie, Oklahoma, has the Lucille Mulhall Room where guests can sleep. To see a picture of the room, and to make reservations, go to *www.stonelioninn.com* or call 405-282-0012.

Other Sources

LeCompte, Mary Lou. *Cowgirls of the Rodeo: Pioneer Professional Athletes.* 36-69. Champaign: University of Illinois Press, 1993.

"Mulhall." Biographical article, provided by the Oklahoma Historical Society, no further identification.

Olds, Fred. "America's Greatest Horsewoman." Copy of article provided by the Oklahoma Historical Society, no further identification.

Sherr, Lynn and Jurate Kazickas. *Susan B. Anthony Slept Here: A Guide to American Women's Landmarks.* 367, 435. New York: Random House, 1994.

ABOUT THE AUTHOR

Betty Bolté has operated a freelance writing and editing business since 1992. She graduated *summa cum laude* from Indiana University in December 1995, with a BA in English, and a minor in Anthropology. She is a member of the Authors Guild and the Romance Writers of America. She has written more than 45 articles for newspapers and magazines across the country. She wrote two books, in addition to this one, in 2001 for younger audiences: *Jumping* and *Dressage* for The Horse Library published by Chelsea House. She lives on a mini horse farm in Canton, Georgia with her husband, father, and two children.

INDEX

Agar, Adam, 207-208
Alferez, Enrique, 223
Ambrister, Robert, 9, 15
Anna, Santa, 29, 32
Ballew, Bud, 252
Bedell, Norman, 98
Bennett, Grace Hardinge, 131
Bennett, John H., 145
Billings, George Newton, 99
Billings, Grace Bedell, 95
Billings, Harlow, 99
Bishop, Ellarene, 99
Boyd, Belle, 116, 122, 124-125, 128, 130-135, 140
Boyd, Benjamin, 133
Boyd, Glenn, 129
Boyd, Isabelle, 129
Boyd, Mary, 116, 129
Boyd, Mary Rebecca Glenn, 129
Boyd, Mrs. Samuel, 129
Boyd, William, 129
Brown, David, 7
Brown, Frances, 7
Brown, Milly Cooper, 1, 7
Brown, Robert, 6

Burnett, Tom, 252
Bynum, Albert, 174
Bynum, Asa, 174, 177
Bynum, Isaac, 174
Bynum, Maud, 174
Bynum, Murty A., 174
Bynum, Winnie Mae, 174
Caw Indians, 44
Cooper, Captain Braxton, 1
Cooper, Milly, 1, 7
Cooper, Sarshell, 6
Cooper's Fort, Missouri, 2
Cornelius, Sarah Kathryn, 175
Creek Indians, 19
Crouse, Catharine, 145
Crouse, Charles, 139
Crouse, Ellen, 139
Crouse, Frances, 139
Crouse, George, 145
Crouse, George W., 139, 145
Crouse, Laura, 145
Crouse, Martha, 138, 139
Crouse, Mary, 145
Crouse, Nancy, 137, 140, 145-146, 148
Crouse, Phoebe, 145
Crouse, Rebecca, 138, 145
Davis, John, 112
Davis, Sam, 112, 114-115
Donahue, Pat, 208
Donner, Elizabeth, 44
Donner, George, 61
Donner, Jacob, 44, 50

Donner Party, 44
Donner, Tamsen, 44
Eberhart, Mrs. Ben, 230
Elliot, Milt, 55
Ellsworth, Annie, 34-36
Ellsworth, Edward A., 39
Ellsworth, Henry Leavitt, 38, 41
Ellsworth, Henry W., 39
Ellsworth, Nancy Allen Goodrich, 38
End-of-the-snake, 75-76, 80
Farragut, Admiral David Glasgow, 193
Fergus, Ernestine, 113-114
Fergus, George Gray, 113
Fergus, John G., 113
Forrest, General Nathan Bedford, 151, 153, 157, 162
Fort Cooper, Missouri, 5-6
Fort Gadsden, Florida, 15
Fort Gibson, Oklahoma, 15
Fort St. Marks, Florida, 9, 13-14
Francis, Mallee, 9, 14
Francis, Milly, 16-17, 19
Francis the Prophet, 9, 14-15
Freeman, Minnie, 225, 228, 230-232
Fuller, Augusta Morrison, 240
Fuller, Edward, 240
Fuller, Edwina Fay, 234, 241
Fuller, Fay, 234, 236, 240-243
Fuller, Robert E., 240
Gagliardi, Thommaso, 189, 193
Gardner, Abigail, 64, 81, 84
Gardner, Eliza M., 81
Gardner, Frances M. Smith, 81

Gardner, Mary M., 81
Gardner, Rowland, 81
Geronimo, 255
Goodell, Andrew, 99
Hadjo, Hillis, 14
Hammond, Byrd, 131
Hammond, Colonel John Swainton, 131
Hammond, John Edmund, 131
Hammond, Marie Isabelle, 131
Hardinge, Samuel Wylde, 130
High, Nat, 131
Hitchcock, Colonel Ethan Allen, 15
Houston, Sam, 32
Hoxie, Richard Leveridge, 193
Inkpaduta, 65, 70, 74-75, 78-80
Jackson, General Andrew, 10, 14
Johnson, Christopher Bullard, 158
Johnson, Mattie Forrest, 158
Kyle, Colonel Robert, 113
Kyle, Mary Kate Patterson Davis Hill, 113-114
Lewis, Frank, 61
Lillie, Gordon, 253
Lincoln, Abraham, 95, 97, 99, 101-102, 139, 141, 178, 183, 185-186
Luce, Albert, 81-82
Luce, Amanda, 81-82
Luce, Harvey, 81
Marble, Margaret Ann, 81
Matowaken, 81
McCormick, J.W., 252
McKrimmon, Duncan, 12, 14, 19
McLeod, Hugh, 22-23, 26-28
Mills, Clark, 181-183, 186, 191

Morse, Samuel F.B., 40
Mulhall, Agnes, 250
Mulhall, Charley, 250
Mulhall, Colonel Zach, 250
Mulhall, Logan, 250
Mulhall, Lucille, 244, 246-247, 250-252, 254-256
Mulhall, Madolyn, 251
Mulhall, Marmaduke, 251
Mulhall, Mary Agnes, 250
Mulhall, Mildred, 251
Murphree, Aaron, 165-166
Murphree, Arminda, 166-168, 173
Murphree, Bailey, 172
Murphree, Ben, 172
Murphree, Celia, 170
Murphree, Elijah, 172
Murphree, Isaac, 168, 172
Murphree, Levi, 172
Murphree, Mary Matilda, 166, 173
Murphree, Sarah Easley, 165, 172
Murphree, Solomon, 174
Murphree, William, 172
Murphree, Winnie Mae, 165, 167, 172, 176
Murphy, John M., 61
Neuhauser, Mrs. Edward, 241
Noble, Lydia, 81
Olmstead, A.P., 208
Pagano, Joseph, 99
Patterson, Charles, 104
Patterson, Dr. Hugh, 104
Patterson, Ellen T., 111
Patterson, Everand Meade, 111

Patterson, Hugh, 104
Patterson, James, 104
Patterson, Margaret, 104
Patterson, Mary Kate, 103, 107, 111, 113-114
Patterson, Robert, 103
Pawnee Bill, 253
Penney, E.B., 231
Picton, Dr. J.P, 222
Pope, Colonel Solomon Lewis, 29
Pope, Henry Bainbridge, 29
Pope, Marcellus Troutman, 30
Pope, Solomon Lewis II, 30
Ream, Cynthia Ann "Mary", 178, 180-181, 186, 188, 190, 195, 198
Ream, Lavinia Ellen, 178, 190
Ream, Lavinia McDonald, 190
Ream, Robert II, 190
Ream, Robert Lee, 190
Ream, Vinnie, 180, 186, 190, 195, 198
Reed, James, 43, 51, 59
Reed, James J., 43, 51, 58
Reed, Margaret, 54-55
Reed, Patty, 43, 51
Reed, Thomas, 43
Reed, Virginia, 43, 60, 62
Reneau, Albert H., 174
Reneau, Arta C., 174
Reneau, Delia, 174
Reneau, John C., 174, 177
Reneau, Myrtle, 174
Reneau, Retty A., 174
Reneau, Sarah Louise, 174
Rogers, Will, 244, 248, 251, 255

Ross, David, 99
Rousseau, General L. Harrison, 112
Sansom, Anne, 150
Sansom, Emma, 150, 153, 155-156, 158, 161-163
Sansom, Jennie, 150-151, 155-156
Sansom, Joe, 156
Sansom, John, 156
Sansom, Lamila Barfield Vann, 156
Sansom, Liza, 156
Sansom, Martha, 158
Sansom, Mary, 156, 166-168
Sansom, Micajah, 156
Sansom, Orren, 156
Sansom, Rufus, 156
Sansom, Tom, 156
Sansom, William, 155
Sharp, Albert, 82
Sharp, Casville, 82
Shelley, James, 208
Shelley, John, 208-209
Shelley, Kate, 200, 205, 207-210, 212-215
Shelley, Margaret, 201, 208, 212
Shelley, Mayme, 201-204, 208-210
Shelley, Michael, 208
Silcott, Jane, 87, 89, 91, 93
Silcott, John, 92-93
Sioux Indians, 44, 66-68, 76, 78, 80
Smiley, Amanda, 98
Smith, Roswell C., 39
Streight, Colonel Abel, 150, 157
Ta-moot-sin (Chief Timothy), 91
Thatcher, Elizabeth, 81

Troutman, Bainbridge, 27
Troutman, Hiram, 22
Troutman, Joanna, 20-22, 30-33
Troutman, John, 27, 30
Troutman, Marcellus, 30
Van Bergen, Martin, 252
Van Bergen, William Logan, 252
Van Trump, Philemon, 235, 240
Vinson, W.G., 30
von Briesen, Fritz, 241
von Briesen, Hans, 241
Ward, Lt. Col. William, 6
Willard, Frances E., 209
Williams, Baylis, 43
Williams, Eliza, 43
Winnebago Indians, 190
Wood, Ed, 206-208
Woodruff, Robbie, 112
Woodruff, Willie, 112
Wright, Jenny, 216
Wright, Sophie Bell, 216, 221
Wyeth, Dr. John Allen, 157
Yankton Sioux Indians, 81